THE DAY-STAR.

THE

DAY-STAR

OF

AMERICAN FREEDOM;

OR

THE BIRTH AND EARLY GROWTH

OF

TOLERATION,

IN

THE PROVINCE OF MARYLAND:

WITH

A SKETCH OF THE COLONIZATION UPON THE CHESAPEAKE AND ITS TRIBUTARIES, PRECEDING THE REMOVAL OF THE GOVERNMENT FROM ST. MARY'S TO ANNAPOLIS;

AND

A Glimpse of the Numbers and General State of Society, of the Religion and Legislation, of the Life and Manners of the Men, who Worshipped in the Wilderness, at the First Rude Altar of Liberty.

BY GEORGE LYNN-LACHLAN DAVIS,

OF THE BAR OF BALTIMORE.

NEW YORK:

C. SCRIBNER, 145, NASSAU STREET.

1855.

W. H. TINSON, STEREOTYPER. GEO. RUSSELL & CO., PRINTERS.

DEDICATED

TO

THE STATE.

Καὶ γὰρ ἡ πατρὶς ἀρχή τίς ἐστι τῆς ἑκάστου γενέσεως, ὥσπερ καὶ ὁ πατήρ.— PORPHYRY.

. . . . *Τῇ τοῦ Θεοῦ διαταγῇ* . . . — ST. PAUL.

PREFACE.

The papers, I will cite, are, most of them, taken from the Archives, at Annapolis, and at London. Those at the Capital of my State, may be seen in the Executive Chamber, in the Armory, in the Hall of the Court of Appeals, in the Land Office, or in the Office of the Register of Wills. And the documents transmitted to me, were obtained, through the aid of an Index, from the English State-Paper Office.

For the sake of brevity, I will generally omit the depository. The two Records designated by A. B. & H., and by Q., can be consulted, in the Land Office. Where the "No." of the Liber is simply given, the citation has been made from the same office. The "Laws," and "Judgments" belong to the Court of Appeals; and are kept, either in the Hall, or in the Armory. In all other cases, the nature of the subject will indicate the place, from which the paper is taken.

The Index, which has aided me, in sketching the Revolution of 1689, was presented to our Historical Society. It is the gift of my generous countryman, Mr. Peabody, of London ; and the key to a rich store-house of documents and facts, preserved at the great city, from which so many of our forefathers came.

To Mr. Jas. Frisby Gordon, and Doct. Fisher, of Kent ; to Mr. Benj. Ed. Gantt, of Anne-Arundel ; to Messrs. Palmer, and Harrison, of Queen Anne's ; to Messrs. Hopkins, and Donoven, of Talbot ; to Mr. Wm. A. Jarboe, of Prince George's ; to Col. Wm. A. Spencer, and the Hon. Jas. Murray, of Annapolis ; I beg leave to express my thanks, for their polite attention, during my examination of the Archives, in the offices, they respectively occupy. To most of them, am I further indebted for communications addressed me, as marks of their courtesy, in reply to a great variety of inquiries. And my acknowledgments are due to the memory, also, of Owen Norfolk, the late clerk at Upper-Marlborough.

I am under an additional obligation to the librarians, and other officers, in various parts of this State, for the privilege extended me, as an author, of consulting any of the books in their custody. Nor can I fail to confess my sense of gratitude, for the interest so generously manifested in the success of all my researches, by many other gentlemen of Maryland, especially by the members of the Bar, and of the Bench, not only in the communication of important facts and suggestions, but also in the loan of valuable private manuscripts. I may here venture to individualize the Hon. John Carroll Le Grand, Saml. Tyler, Esq., Prof. Evert M. Topping, Wm. Meade Addison, Esq., Prof. Saml. Chew, Hon. E. Louis Lowe, Doct. Peregrine Wroth, Rev. Saml. R. Gordon, Jas. E. Barroll, Esq., Prof. George Fenwick, and Genl. Thos. F. Bowie.

And there are a few personal friends not named in this Preface, nor confined altogether to my own sex, whose companionship has occasionally lightened my labor; whose bright sympathies have shed a sun-shine over the heart, in the hour of toilsome solitude; whose aid, and whose many kind offices, will be sweetly, and sincerely remembered.

CONTENTS.

THE DAY-STAR.

CHAPTER I.

Toleration—Its Logical Relations—Its History cannot yet be properly written.

The march of the mind is slow. Of Islamism, the faith for twelve centuries of a fifth part of the whole human race, no real history, it is sad to think, has ever been written; and the most profound men of Europe confess their ignorance of the subject. It also admits of the gravest doubt, whether we yet have, in the truest and most comprehensive sense, a history of Christianity. And it is vain to hope, in the present state of knowledge, for a satisfactory history of Toleration.

Notwithstanding a regard for the rights of conscience, the laws of our own nation have always evinced a greater sympathy for the Christian than for any other form of belief; while no government has existed without some kind of religious theory; nor has any state, in modern times, at periods even of the wildest anarchy, gone far enough to deny its own ethical nature, or reject that element which constitutes the ground-work and condition of its being.

The Church of no Christian country, on the other hand, is prepared, either upon the Protestant, or upon any other basis, to acknowledge the supremacy of the State, or surrender[1] the jurisdiction it exercises over questions of faith and ethics—questions, which touch the very heart of humanity, and connect us with the invisible world; but work, at the same time, such deep changes in states and empires—having occasioned more

[1] The English Church may be oppressed, or enslaved. But it is a great mistake to suppose she has ever acknowledged the supremacy of the Civil Magistrate. See Magna Charta, the Works of Lord Coke, and the late Writings of the Rt. Rev. Doct. Philpott, of the See of Exeter.

bloodshed, since the martyrdom of St. Stephen (to say nothing of the church controversy, which now, alas! involves the European nations in a fresh conflict) than any of the subjects, which ever engage the attention either of kings or of courts, of cabinets or of parliaments.

The antagonism between the State and the Church, under the existing order of things, may not, indeed, be observed by the ordinary eye. It may apparently sleep, for a season, or for a century. But it is not the less real; and not the less destined, sooner or later, to unfold itself, in all its terrific energy. The advocates of Toleration will then be ready to proclaim, that atheism is the proper fundamental principle of the State; and its opponents, that faith is the foundation of ethics, that the notion of a perfect state implies a church of the same character, that the one is but identical with the other, and that under a more beneficent arrangement of Providence, a higher law of society, and a nobler system of civilization, the identity will be fully and triumphantly revealed. Before the termination of this contest (probably the most momentous, if not the most bloody, which man will be called upon to endure), it will be impossible to find the central-point involved in the great problem of Toleration; or to grasp it, in all its highest logico-historical relations.

CHAPTER II.

The Visible Influence of Ideas—The Charm of External History—Illustrations from Islamism, from Christianity, and from Toleration

Yet Islamism has undoubtedly a meaning. Of its external history, do we also know something. Amid the fiery sands and deserts of Arabia, a thought strikes the mind of a man. To him, it is a vision; to us, a small cloud upon the horizon, destined to overspread the firmament. In the one, we see the image, and the hand of God; in the other, are locked up the living forces of nature. Out of the brain of a wild, but earnest son of the wilderness, springs forth, with the rapidity of magic, a vast and magnificent empire; having its strong and impregnable centre in the East, but extending its dominion to the very confines of the West; clad, indeed, with all the terrors of the sword, but deriving its original strength from the simple words, he had uttered; the grandest and boldest embodiment, (however imperfect,) we have so far witnessed, of the *identity* (if I may tread upon forbidden ground[1]) of the temporal with the spiritual authority; at one moment, threatening to absorb the Christian nations of Europe; at another communicating to their civilization that impulse, which will be felt through all ages! a rich, and gorgeous picture! perplexing, it is true, the judgment of the historical critic; but dazzling the imagination, elevating the fancy, and (may I add?) purifying the heart.

In spite, also, of the little that is known of the higher relations, or the logical harmonies of ecclesiastical history, there is something which touches a still deeper spring in the simple and short story of the Cross—of the visible struggle of Christianity, during the first three centuries, with the Paganism of a great empire—of the mild and serene triumph of the church, at the end of that period, amid the shocks and convulsions of society, over all the phy-

[1] If Newman and Ranke touch this subject with so much caution, an unwillingness in myself to go beyond a mere suggestion, indicates no affectation of modesty.

sical, intellectual, and other powers of the civilized world. From the Crusades to the present, from childhood to hoary age, over the dream of the virgin, and the meditation of the matron, over men of every taste and of every type, it has exerted a magical influence. This moment, I study it, with a more passionate fondness, than "The Arabian Nights," or the most truthful and enchanting picture, the hand of man has sketched, either of domestic manners, or of Oriental magnificence and renown. There is nothing approaching it, upon the pages of the historical record—nothing, in the glory of Grecian combatants, or the march of Roman legions—in living, or in dying gladiators; or victorious generals, whose returning "chariot-wheels" were "graced" by kings "in captive bonds."

The Crescent and the Cross have, each of them, a charm. They represent the two great historical Ideas; they mark the two grand epochs in the destiny of the human race. As the fallen column, amid the ruins of the Acropolis, retains the traces of a high creative art, so man, with all his grossness, still proclaims the divinity of his original nature, by the interest he manifests in the contest of the intellectual with the physical forces; by the sympathy he feels for the spiritual world; by the sacrifice he so joyfully suffers, for the sake of his conscience; by the pride he exhibits at the triumph of a cherished faith; and by the pleasure he derives from the study of those ideas, which have wielded their influence over any considerable portion of society. His *ideality* is the secret of that true historic dignity, which belongs to the colonization of America. Scarcely a settlement, or a colony was founded, which cannot, more or less, be traced to the agency of some religious idea. And the remark includes the landing of the Pilgrims, at St. Mary's, in the year 1634. It forms the key to the earliest history of the province—the pivot to the primitive policy and legislation of the State—and the centre of so much that is interesting in the traditions and recollections, which have been handed down to our own generation. The idea, which our ancestors brought with them to the forests of Maryland, was apparently feeble, in the beginning. But it soon began to show its strength; and like all ideas having vitality, it was progressive. The acorn has since become an oak; the fountain a majestic river. Though it seems to be but half developed (for Toleration is yet without a strict definition, or a symbol), it has already, under a variety of shapes, but all of them substantially the same, become an active element in the religious and political life of a great and colossal confederacy. Judging from the past, it is destined to occupy a still wider field, to over-run other countries, to revolutionize distant nations, and to achieve a greater, a more glorious conquest over the human mind. If we may speak from its visible results, it would be but just to say, its career has so far been bright and hopeful. Viewing it from the Anglo-American side, from the popular theory of religious liberty, we cannot feel too grateful for the blessings, it has conferred; for the prospect, it presents to other portions of humanity. Its developments, indeed, I cannot give; its history, in the proper sense, I cannot write; for that involves relations of a logical sort, which no one living can state upon any of the received hypotheses either of Europe, or of America. But we have much information respecting its external history; something also will I tell of its origin and early growth in this country; nor do I disguise the pride a Marylander must feel, in sketching the following facts. And I think, in the course of this brief narrative, I will be able to suggest a solution to some of the problems which now engross the attention of the nation. Who were the originators of the idea? and what was their faith? are but two of the questions I am so often asked. Addressed by respectable persons, tortured with inquiries upon those and other interesting points, I am urged to speak. And the settlement of open questions in the history of this continent, is surely a matter of no trifling consideration in the present state of the national mind, giving such striking indications of excitement in every quarter, from the St. Lawrence to the Pacific. Most gladly, then, if I could, would I do the state some service; and I hope at a future day to give a perfectly satisfactory answer. But my life is one of accidents; and the history I am writing of the colonization of Maryland, may demand the unsparing toil of several more years. From my portfolio I will, therefore, take a few papers, and at once respond; from the shadows of my solitary chamber, from the dry and dusty records, from the living oracles of the past, I will now address the millions of my countrymen.

CHAPTER III.

The Toleration Secured by the Charter for Maryland.

THE charter[1] was a compact between a member of the English, and a disciple of the Roman church; between an Anglo-Catholic king and a Roman Catholic prince; between Charles the First of England, and Cecilius, the second baron of Baltimore, and the first lord proprietary of Maryland. To the confessors of each faith, it was the pledge of religious freedom. If not the form, it had the spirit and substance of a *concordat*, in the sense quite as strong, as any of those earlier charters of the English Crown, to which the chief priest of Rome was, in any respect, a party. This is the inference faithfully drawn from a view of the instrument itself; from a consideration of the facts and circumstances attending the grant; and

[1] The Charter was given in 1632. There is a copy in Bacon's Laws, in Bozman's Maryland, and in Hazard's Collections.

from a study of the various interpretations, essays, and histories, of the many discourses, and other publications, which have appeared upon this prolific theme. It accounts for the prohibition of every construction inconsistent with the "*true Christian religion*[1]"—an expression coming from the lips of an English king, and resembling a clause in the first charter for the *Anglo-Catholic* colony of Virginia[2]

[1] The words in the English copy (see Sec. 22 of the Charter) are "God's holy and true Christian religion;" in the Latin (see Bacon and Hazard), "Sacrosancta Dei et vera Christiana religio." To Mr. Brantz Mayer (see his Calvert and Penn) is due the credit of pointing out a grammatical inaccuracy in the English translation. We are indebted to Mr. S. F. Streeter also (see his Maryland Two Hundred Years Ago) for a learned note of a subsequent date. The former's translation is, "God's holy rights, and the true Christian religion;" the latter's, "the holy service of God, and true Christian religion;" and my own, "the most sacred things of God, and the true Christian religion." Mr. Mayer, indeed, suggests, in a note, the agreement of "sacrosancta" with "negotia;" and gives no sufficient reason, it strikes me, for substituting "rights" for "things." See his text, p. 28. The substitute is too narrow; and I cannot, therefore, adopt it.

[2] In the Charter of 1606 occur, "the true word and service of God and Christian faith;" in the one of 1609, "the true worship of God and Christian religion;" and in the orders of 1619 and

—but, in a grant to the *Roman Catholic* proprietary, intended, doubtless, as a simple security for the members of the English church. It suggests the reason also, why the obligation to establish the religion of Englishmen was omitted in the case of Maryland; but expressly or tacitly imposed, either by the charters or by the orders given to most, if not all, of the other Anglo-American colonies.[1] It is not less in harmony with the supposition of King Charles's regard for the rights of his Anglo-Catholic brethren, who subsequently came to St.

1620, "the true religion and service of God." These expressions clearly refer to the religion of the English Church in a strictly exclusive sense. See Henning's Collection, and the preceding publication of Mr. Streeter, pp. 71–76. "The true Christian faith, now professed in the Church of England," is a clause in the letters patent to Sir Walter Raleigh. See Streeter, p. 73. See also, in Streeter, the Charters to Sir Edmund Plowden for New Albion, and to Sir Ferdinando Gorges for Maine. "Worship and religion of Christ," in the 4th sec. of the Maryland Charter, doubtless refers to the English Church.

[1] The Virginia Charter of 1609 virtually excluded the Roman Catholics; so did the one for New England to Fernando Gorges and other persons, in 1621. See Streeter. Other cases could be cited.

Mary's, than with that generally admitted sincerity of Lord Baltimore, which cannot be reconciled to the notion of his accepting a grant directly opposed to the principles, or to the practice of his own faith. It is supported by the fact, that the object of the Calverts, in asking for the charter, was to found a colony, including the members, respectively, of the English, and of the Roman church—an object which, we cannot doubt, was known to the king, who signed the instrument. And it is fully confirmed by the action of the provincial legislature—the best commentary upon the spirit of the charter—and by one of the first judicial decisions still preserved upon the records. Within a short period after the landing of the Pilgrims, an act was passed, declaring, that "Holy Church" should enjoy "all her rights;" and, a year later, it was followed by another of the same purport.[1] These words were clearly taken from the

[1] The Act of 1639 declares that, "Holy Church, within this province, shall have all her rights and liberties;" the one of 1640, that, "Holy Church, within this province, shall have and enjoy all her rights, liberties, and franchises, wholly and without blemish." See Bacon, Bozman, and many other authorities. A bill also of

great charters of the English Crown, in the days of the Normans and of the Plantagenets;[1] and, in both cases, the term "*Holy*" included the English as well as the Roman church.[2] We will

1639 says, "Holy Church, within this province, shall have all her rights, liberties, and immunities, safe, whole, and inviolable in all things."

[1] The Charter of King John stipulates that the English Church "shall be free, and shall have her whole rights and her liberties inviolable;" the first one of Henry the Third, that she shall "be free," and "have her whole rights and liberties inviolable;" the second of the same king, that "she shall be free," and "have her whole rights and her liberties inviolable;" the third, that she "shall be free, and shall have her whole rights and her liberties inviolable;" and the first of Edward the First, that she "shall be free," and "have her whole rights and liberties inviolable."

[2] It is surprising to think, how some of our historians have been embarrassed in the attempt to interpret the two acts of the Assembly. The close resemblance of our early legislation to the charters I have cited does not seem to have occurred to Chalmers, Hawks, Allen, and many others. If the case of the Rev. Francis Fitzherbert, in another note, be any authority, the "doctors of the Church" were by no means "puzzled." There is also a striking analogy between our primitive forms or precedents, and the expressions contained in the charter of King John. Compare, for instance, the oath of the Privy Councillor, in 1648, to "delay or deny right" to "none," with the fortieth section of that charter.

see that "*Holy Church*" was used, at a subsequent period, in a much more comprehensive sense. But neither in the early English charters, nor in the two preceding acts of the Assembly, did the words secure anything but the rights of the Anglican, and of the Roman Catholic. In the case of Lieut. Wm. Lewis, the Roman Catholic, convicted, in 1638, of violating a proclamation, by improperly engaging in religious controversy, and thereby disturbing the "peace" of the colony; the main ground of the offence consisted, in his inveighing against the Protestants, for reading a book[1] "*allowed*" by "*the State of England.*" Such

Each section of the charter has, indeed, been called a statute. And the law of 1639, including the section relating to the Church, may be regarded as a series of acts partaking of the nature of a Magna Charta. Certain it is, that, in the Charter of King John, "Holy Church" occurs in a sense distinct from "Holy Roman Church," as well as from "English Church." It can bear but one interpretation. Both in the early charters, and in the acts of our Assembly, it clearly includes the Anglican not less than the Roman Catholics.

[1] The case of Lewis has so often been published (see, *e.g.*, Bozman, vol. 2, pp. 83–85, and 596–598), that it is necessary only to add, the proclamation of Governor Calvert prohibited " all unsea-

was the test of an Anglo-Catholic's rights, under the earliest practice of the government. Such was the doctrine in the case which has been cited; such the opinion of Mr. Secretary Lewger, a justice of the Supreme Court; and such the decision of Leonard Calvert, the lieutenant general or governor, and the chief justice of the province. "*Holy*," as well as "*Catholic*," we know also, is used in creeds common to the English and to the Roman church. And "*Catholic*" is a term not unfrequently applied, upon the provincial records, to the Church of England.[1] The little chapel also, near the Fort at St. Mary's, the place for the worship of the Anglo-Catholic colonists before the arrival of any of their ministers, and

sonable disputations, in point of religion, tending to the disturbance of the public peace and quiet of the colony, and to the opening of faction in religion." See 2 Bozman, p. 83.

[1] In 1642, "the Protestant Catholics of Maryland" are mentioned upon the Records—intended, no doubt, for the members of the English Church. See their petition to the Assembly, in 2 Bozman, p. 199. In some, also, of the early wills, "Catholic" is applied to the Church of England. See the one of Thos. Banks, in 1684, Lib. G., p. 126.

given by most writers to the Protestants, was probably not their property exclusively, but erected with the joint funds or contributions of the Roman and of the Anglican Catholics. The key to it was seized, in 1642, by Doctor Gerrard, a prominent Roman Catholic,[1] and upon the ground of *some claim*, if we may judge from an expression in the decision against him. In the proposal, about the same year, for a transfer of the premises to Lord Baltimore (an arrangement not immediately, if ever at all, effected), another Roman Catholic gentleman was the ostensible owner or representative of the title. And there is evidence to show, that at a very early period, the graveyard was the usual burial-place of the Roman Catholics.[2] Some also of the colonists, who held land, under Doctor Gerrard, as the lord of St. Clement's Manor, as

[1] See the case of Thos. Gerrard, in 2 Bozman, pp. 199–200.

[2] Such, it seems, was the fact, from the will of John Lloyd, of St. Mary's—a Roman Catholic, who expressed the wish to be interred "in ye ordinary burying-place, in St. Mary's chapel-yard." See his will of 1658, in Lib. S., 1658 to 1662, Judgments, pp. 74–75.

well as the Doctor's wife,[1] were Protestants. And he, and other Roman Catholics, it is not unreasonable to suppose, were partly instrumental in building this little temple, in token of the concord[2] between the English and the Roman Catholic; and where each, at his own appropriate hour, might offer up his sacrifice to the Most High.

Faithfully did Cecilius, the proprietary, execute the pledge he had given to the members of the English church. How intoxicating is the taste of power! How apt are we to forget the obligation we owe to those whom we command! How easy was it for the proprietary, in an obscure and remote part of the world, beyond the immediate eye of the Crown,

[1] The case of the Rev. Francis Fitzherbert develops the faith of Doctor Gerrard and his wife.

[2] My theory respecting the object and ownership of the chapel, is by no means essential to the support of the interpretation given to the charter. But under every aspect, it is, in itself, highly probable. And I suggest it as one of the evidences that the harmony existed, barring a few individual cases, as a living reality, independently even of the action of the Proprietary's government. For negotiations respecting the purchase, see Bozman, vol. 2, pp. 263, and 627–628.

to commit acts of petty cruelty and oppression towards those who differed with him on points of faith, not only by excluding them from civil offices but also in many other respects! How often do we deny to others, what we have so earnestly claimed for ourselves! And how great is the reproach to human nature—to peasants as well as princes, in that and in every other age—arising from the disregard so often manifested for the obligation of promises, or for the sacredness of treaties! The singular fidelity with which the second baron of Baltimore kept his pledge, presents one of the best examples upon the record, one of the purest lessons of history, one of the strongest claims to the gratitude of Maryland, and to the admiration of the world.

CHAPTER IV.

The Toleration under the first Governor.

SUCH is the meaning of the charter historically interpreted; and such the earliest principle and practice of the government—freedom to the Anglican and freedom to the Roman Catholic—a freedom of conscience, not allowed but exacted. A freedom, however, of a wider sort springs forth at the birth of the colony—not demanded by that instrument, but permitted by it—not graven upon the tables of stone, or written upon the pages of the statute-book—but conceived in the very bosom of the proprietary, and of the original Pilgrims—not a formal or constructive, but a living freedom—a freedom of the most practical sort. It is the freedom, which it remained for them, and for them alone, either to grant or to deny—a freedom embracing within its range, and protecting under its banner, all those who were believers in JESUS

CHRIST. And the grant of this freedom is that which has placed the proprietary among the first law-reformers of the world, and Maryland in advance of every State upon the continent. Our ancestors had seen the evils of intolerance; they had tasted the bitter cup of persecution. Happy is he whose moral sense has not been corrupted by bigotry, whose heart is not hardened by misfortune, whose soul (the spring of generous impulse) has never been dried up by the parching adversities of life! They brought with them, in "The Ark," and "The Dove," the elements of that liberty they had so much desired, themselves, in the Old World, and which to others in the New, of a different faith, they were too good and too just to deny. Upon the banks of the St. Mary's, in the soil of Maryland, amid the wilderness of America, they planted that seed which has since become a tree of life to the nation, extending its branches and casting its shadows across a whole continent. The records have been carefully searched. No case of persecution occurred during the administration of Governor Leonard Calvert, from the foundation of the settlement at St. Mary's to the year 1647. His policy included the humblest as well as the most exalted; and his maxim was, PEACE TO ALL—PROSCRIPTION OF NONE.[1] RELIGIOUS LIBERTY was a VITAL PART of the earliest common-law of the province.

[1] The inference from a careful search of the Records is confirmed by the testimony of Langford, whose "Refutation of Babylon's Fall" was published very soon after the battle of 1655; and by the authority of Bancroft and other historians. Mr. Bancroft says (see vol. 1, p. 257) that the government, in conformity with strict and *repeated* injunctions, had never given disturbance to any persons in Maryland "for matter of religion." The Protestant declaration of 1650, also contains evidence independently of that, which relates to the Act of 1649.

CHAPTER V.

Toleration Implied in the Official Oath.

At the date of the charter, Toleration existed in the heart of the proprietary. And it appeared, in the earliest administration of the affairs of the province. But an oath was soon prepared by him, including a pledge from the governor and the privy counsellors, "directly or indirectly," to "trouble, molest, or discountenance" no "person whatever," in the province, "professing to believe in Jesus Christ." Its date is still an open question —some writers supposing it was imposed in 1637; and others, in 1648. I am inclined to think the oath of the latter was but "an augmented edition"[1]

[1] See Brantz Mayer's "Calvert and Penn," pp. 46–47; Chalmers's Annals; and the authorities quoted by Mr. Mayer. See also Langford's "Refutation of Babylon's Fall." I do not, however, conceive there is anything material in the *exact* date, or in the *formal* imposition.

of the one in the former year. The grant of the charter marks the era of a special Toleration. But the earliest practice of the government presents the first; the official oath, the second; the action of the Assembly in 1649, the third, and, to advocates of a republican government, the most important phasis, in the history of the general Toleration. The oath of 1648 is worthy of attention, in another particular. It contained a special pledge, in favor of the Roman Catholics—a feature, which might have been deemed requisite, in consideration of the fact, that the proprietary had appointed a Protestant gentleman[1] for the post of lieutenant-general, or governor. Some also of the privy counsellors were of the same faith.

[1] This view is confirmed by Langford, and accepted by Streeter, who certainly manifests no partiality for the proprietary.

CHAPTER VI.

The Assembly of 1649—Kent and St. Mary's Represented—Sketch of their Early History—Passage of the Toleration Act.

THE little provincial parliament of Maryland assembled, at St. Mary's, in the month of April,[1] during the year 1649. This was about fifteen years after the landing of the Pilgrims, under Governor Calvert; about thirty later than the settlement of the Puritans at Plymouth; and more than forty, subsequently to the arrival of the Anglo-Catholics at Jamestown, in Virginia. The members of the Assembly at St. Mary's met in a spirit of moderation but seldom the characteristic of a dominant party. The province was at peace with the aboriginal tribes within its limits. The unhappy contest with Col. Wm. Clayborne had

[1] The Assembly met about the 14th of April, according to the present calendar, or the 2d of that month, Old Style. For the Julian, or Old Style, see 2 Bozman, p. 384.

been virtually terminated; the rebellions of Capt. Richard Ingle, and other Protestant enemies, effectively suppressed; the reins of government recovered; and the principles of order once more established. Governor Calvert, the chief of the Maryland Pilgrims, after a trying, but heroic, and honorable administration, had died, amid the prayers and blessings of his friends, without a stain upon his memory. Thos. Green had, also, for a short period, been the governor. And the principal key of authority was then held by Capt. Wm. Stone.

The Assembly was composed of the governor, the privy counsellors and the burgesses. In many particulars, its model was not unlike that of the primitive parliaments of England.[1] The governor and the privy counsellors were appointed by Cecilius, the feudal prince or proprietary of the province; the burgesses, who were chosen by the freemen, represented the democratic element in the original constitution of Maryland. The dele-

[1] The Assembly was sometimes called "Parliament." See the Records; also 2 Bosman, p. 185, note.

gates were sent by Kent and by St. Mary's, the only two counties at that time within the limits of the principality; the former upon the east, the latter upon the west side of "The Great Bay." And while there is no reason for asserting the want of harmony upon the business of this Assembly, it is a remarkable fact, that for more than two centuries the most strongly marked differences have existed between the shores of the Chesapeake, not only of a geographical, but also of a political character.

Kent, in the midst of many sad reverses, had grown out of a settlement founded as early as 1630, by Col. Clayborne, in the spirit of a truly heroic adventure, under the jurisdiction established at Jamestown, and during the administration (it is supposed) of Governor Harvey, upon an island of the Chesapeake called Kent, but then the "Isle of Kent;"[1] a purchase (to quote the colonel's own

[1] It is supposed by some that the island derived its name from the birthplace of Clayborne. There were families of his name in Westmoreland and York. But there is no trace of him in Philpot's "Villare," or any other work I have seen relating to Kent. The island, I think, was named in honor of the governor under

words) from "the kings of that country;"[1] and the original centre[2] of the county represented at St. Mary's, though now included within the limits

whose administration, or auspices, the settlement was founded, and who was probably a native of the English county of Kent.

[1] Bozman, vol. ii. pp. 67 and 582.

[2] The seat of Clayborne's settlement was at Kent Point. There also was the "Mill," several of which (that is, windmills) can still be seen. There is not a single water-fall upon the island, and the records mention the "vane," and other things, which prove the wind was the motive power.

Near the "Mill" was Fort Kent. Fort Crayford stood near Craney Creek, now a pond, and is frequently noticed upon the old records at Chestertown, especially in the deeds containing the boundary lines to tracts of land. It is not named in any of our histories; but the recorded evidence is as strong as that relating to the site of the other fort.

Kent Fort Manor included Kent Mill and Kent Fort. It was given by the proprietary to Gov. Calvert as a reward for his services in the conquest of the island; but assigned to Capt. Giles Brent, whose family, for many generations, held the title. From the testimony of Mr. Bryan, a soldier of 1776, and at the time of my interview nearly ninety-five years old, I learn that the manor-house was burnt during his childhood; but another, upon the same foundation, soon afterwards built. The spot is easily designated, being but a few hundred yards from the vault, and still nearer to a small clump of old and dwarfish damascene-trees. The

of Queen Anne's[1]—an island still noted for the beauty of its scenery, and the wealth of its waters in fish and fowl; and the only dwelling-place of the colonists upon the eastern shore, at the time of this Assembly; the seat, also, of opulence and elegance at a period anterior to the American Revolution;[2] and represented in the Virginia

piece of a mill-stone, the fragment of an oven-lid, and a few other relics, may now be picked up. In the examination of these interesting localities, I was kindly aided by several intelligent gentlemen, especially by Doctor Samuel Harper, of Easton.

There was a court-house upon the island; the first on the east side of the Chesapeake. It stood, I am inclined to think, upon the eastern part of the island.

The Matapeakes are the only Indians whose residence upon the island, or whose name can be traced. They lived at one time near *Indian* Spring; and at another, in *Matapax* Neck. See my paper presented to the Md. Hist. Society.

[1] The island, first of all, was under the jurisdiction of Virginia; then the subject of contest between Lord Baltimore and Colonel Clayborne; subsequently annexed as a hundred to St. Mary's; and next erected into a county. At a later period, it belonged to Talbot. But before the year 1695, it was again, though for a short time, erected into a county.

[2] See Eddis's Letters—an instructive, well-written volume—where the reader will find an interesting sketch of a visit to the island.

House of Burgesses, before the settlement at St. Mary's;[1] but, above all, distinguished as the first focal point of Anglo-American civilization[2] within the present boundaries of our State.

St. Mary's, which also had been purchased from the Indians—how honorable to the memory of those who took part in that transaction![3]—and

[1] "The Virginians," says Chalmers, "boasted, with their wonted pride, that the colonists of Kent sent burgesses to their Assembly, and were subjected to their jurisdiction, before Maryland had a name." Nor was the boast without foundation. Their early legislative journals (see Henning's Collection) show conclusively, that the island was represented by Capt. Nicholas Martin.

[2] The date of the settlement cannot be accurately given. The Rev. Ethan Allen supposes it was during the year 1629. See Allen's Maryland Toleration, p. 8.

[3] The following extract will show the manner in which Governor Calvert proceeded, soon after his arrival:—

"To make his entry peaceable and safe, he thought fit to present ye Werowance and Wisoes of the town (so they call ye chief men of account among them), with some English cloth (such as is used in trade with ye Indians), axes, hoes, and knives, which they accepted very kindly, and freely gave consent to his company, that he and they should dwell in one part of their town, and reserve the other for themselves: and those Indians that dwelt in that part of ye town which was allotted for ye English, freely left them their houses and some corn that they had begun to plant.

which had borne the appellation of *Augusta-Carolina*,[1] included a territory of thirty miles, extending towards the mouth of the Potomac, and embracing the St. Mary's, which flows into that river. Within this county was also the small city, which had been founded upon the site an abori-

It was also agreed between them, that at ye end of ye harvest, they should have ye whole town, which they did accordingly. And they made mutual promises to each other to live peaceably and friendly together; and if any injury should happen to be done, on any part, that satisfaction should be made for ye same; and thus, on ye 27th day of March, A.D. 1634, ye governor took possession of ye place, and named ye town *St. Maries*.

"There was an occasion that much facilitated their treaty with these Indians, which was this: the Susquehanocks (a warlike people that inhabit between Chesapeake Bay and Delaware Bay) did usually make wars and incursions upon ye neighboring Indians, partly for superiority, partly for to get their women, and what other purchase they could meet with; which the Indians of *Yoacomaco* fearing, had, ye year before our arrival there, made a resolution, for their safety, to remove themselves higher into ye country, where it was more populous, and many of them were gone there when ye English arrived." See "A Relation of Maryland, 1635."

[1] In honor, we may suppose of King Charles. Augusta was not borne by any member of the royal family; nor was Caroline. The former may be regarded as an adjective, or epithet.

ginal village;[1] and which, like the river upon which it stood, derived its beautiful name from the Blessed Virgin; the chief star in a constellation of little settlements and plantations; and for a period of about sixty years, the provincial capital of Maryland—a city of which nothing now remains, deserving the dignity of ruins, and a few relics only are preserved—the records and everything belonging to the government having long since been removed to Annapolis—but a spot still consecrated in the affections of the country—one which is visited upon anniversary and other occasions by the well-bred sons of Maryland, and to which patriots of other States may look with pride and pleasure—where also the pilgrim of the future, in approaching the shrine already dedicated by the voice of history, will ever rejoice to pour out his feelings in expressions of profound gratitude to God.

The principle of compensation for services, it is proper to state, was not adopted by the memorable Assembly of 1649. The only consideration

[1] Yacomico.

allowed the representatives of the freemen, and paid in their usual currency, was twenty-six pounds of tobacco each day—a quantity equivalent to seventy-eight pence in English, or a hundred and fifty-six cents in American money—and intended simply to cover the cost of "their diet," and the "loss of their time." One member, indeed, of the Lower House received a consideration for service, or "trouble;" but three others only ten pounds of tobacco, respectively. The whole "bill of charges," so far, at least, as regards the burgesses, was prepared with a special reference to the exhausted state of the province. And we may suppose, that some of them waived a part even of their right to the little allowance.

The members of our early provincial parliaments, unlike some of their English prototypes, generally, if not always, in entering the House took off their hats. They also stood when they addressed the chair. They seem, indeed, to have been distinguished, for their sense of modesty; and for the strongest sentiments of respect and affection for the person of the proprietary. But they lacked nothing of the spirit, or independence of freemen. They were not under the proprietary's dictation. The legislative annals are full of striking and well-known illustrations of their manhood. If proof were needed, the very letter addressed him, by the Assembly of this year, and published in Bozman's History, would be sufficient.

In the Hall of Edward the Confessor, a picture has been presented of the primitive parliament, by one of England's most accurate historians. The Anglo-Saxon is giving his friendly explanations of the Assembly to the Norwegian stranger. "Haco," says he, "you well know how we call this Assembly?—A *Micel getheaht*,[1] or *Great thought*—a *Witena-gemot*, or *Meeting of the Wise*—and at present it well deserves its name. Our *Redes-men*, or counsellors, the members of the legislature, ponder much before they come together, say little, and write less."[2] May it not, with a still greater truth, be affirmed, that our own early law-givers were the representatives of a great and sublime conception? And judging

[1] From the Anglo-Saxon word, "*micel*" (big), is derived our English surname "*Mitchel*."

[2] Palgrave's History of the Anglo-Saxons, Preface, p. 25.

from the number of wholesome laws enacted in 1649, as well as the shortness of their session (for it did not include twenty-five days), it would seem, the Assembly-men of this year were certainly not very fond of talking or speech-making. It appears also, that some of them, like our Saxon forefathers,[2] could neither read nor write. It can be proved from the records, that two of them, at least, were in the habit of making a signet mark.[3] But did they not leave a mark also upon the country, and upon the world? In depth and earnest-

[1] "I hear," says the Anglo-Saxon, "that amongst the French they designate such assemblies as ours by the name of a '*colloquium*,' or, as we should say, a 'talk'—which they render, in their corrupted romance-jargon, by the word '*parlement;*' and should our '*Witenagemot,*' our '*Micel-getheaht,*' ever cease to be a 'meeting of the wise,' or 'great-thought,' and become a '*parlement,*' or 'great-talk,' it will be worse for England than if a myriad of your northern pirates were to ravish the land from sea to sea." Palgrave, p. 26.

[2] Some even of the Anglo-Saxon kings made their mark. It is doubtful if William the Conqueror could write.

[3] Col. John Price, of the upper, and Mr. John Maunsell, of the lower House: the former a Protestant, the latter a Roman Catholic.

ness, in real dignity and propriety, in profound views of human nature, and in true legislative wisdom, they were not a whit behind those earlier law-givers, who bore the appellation of "The Wise," and whose bright renown has come down to our own age. The laws of King Alfred, so celebrated in the history of English jurisprudence, do not excel the legislation of our own little Assembly, during the dominion of the first proprietary. The principle adopted by the Assembly of this year, respecting the purchase of Indian land-titles, has since been tested a thousand times; and is now a prominent feature in the policy of the federal government. But to the legislators of 1649, was it given, to discharge a much higher task—to execute a much nobler mission—to inaugurate a much greater idea—an idea which had existed in the bosom of the proprietary, and been sanctioned by the earliest practice of the government; but yet awaited a formal confirmation from the Roman Catholic and from the Protestant planters of the province. The time, at length, arrived for them also, to officiate at the altar of religious freedom; and to take their own rank among the foremost spirits of the age. Near the close of the session, within the range of aboriginal villages, and the blaze of Indian council fires, they took counsel, we may suppose, not only of each other, but also of the true "FATHER OF LIGHTS," and then, by a solemn act, they endorsed that policy, which ever since has shed the brightest lustre upon the legislative annals of the province.

CHAPTER VII.

"The Act concerning Religion."

The "Act concerning Religion" (for that is the the title of the law) has already been printed. But it forms so important a link in the chain of this narrative, that its leading provisions should be stated. The design was five-fold:—to guard by an express penalty "*the most sacred things*[1] *of God*;" to inculcate the principle of religious decency and order; to establish, upon a firmer basis, the harmony already existing between the colonists; to secure, in the fullest sense, freedom as well as protection to all believers in Christianity;[2] and to

[1] "Sacrosancta" was used by the Latin fathers (see Andrews and other authorities) for the most sacred things. And such I take to be the sense intended in the writings of English divines and in state papers corresponding with the date of the charter. In this I am confirmed also by the action of the provincial legislature.

[2] Upon the Records of the High Provincial Court is preserved

protect quiet disbelievers against every sort of reproach, or ignominy. In determining the different lines and landmarks, a regard, of course, must be had to the spirit of the charter, to the theological notions of the age, and to the character of the elements, which then composed the population of the province.

a case in which the prisoner, a Roman Catholic priest, vindicated his right under this leading provision of the law. It is, in many respects, a very interesting one, and sheds a great deal of light upon the domestic, social, and religious history of this period. The Act of 1639 included, we have seen, the English and the Roman Church. But the one of 1649 practically gave to the term "holy" a much more comprehensive signification.

In Father Fitzherbert's case, the following are the proceedings of the court, which was held at St. Leonard's Creek, "the 5th of October" O. S. A.D. 1658. Present—Gov. Fendall; Philip Calvert, Esq., Col. Utye, Capt. Stone, and Messrs. Job Chandler and Baker Brooke.

"An information of his lordship's attorney against Francis Fitzherbert, for practising of treason and sedition, and giving out rebellious and mutinous speeches, in this his lordship's province of Maryland, and endeavouring, as far as in him lay, to raise distraction and disturbances in this his lordship's said province.

"1. Francis Fitzherbert did, on ye 24th of August, 1658, traitorously and seditiously, at a general meeting in arms of the people of the upper parts of Patuxent River, to muster, endeavour to seduce, and draw from their religion, the inhabitants there met together.

1. The proprietary had the right upon all doubtful points, to construe the charter in that manner which was most favorable to himself. But no interpretation was allowed inconsistent with the "*Sacrosancta Dei*," and the "*Vera Christiana Religio*"—the former, doubtless, implying a prohibition of the most wicked kind of *blasphemy*, as

"2. He did use the same traitorous and rebellious practice at Newtown on the 30th of August, 1658, the people being met together for ye end aforesaid.

"3. That, by these his traitorous and seditious practices, he hath caused several inhabitants of this province to refuse to appear at musters; that they shall thereby be incapable of defending the peace and liberty of ye inhabitants of this his lordship's province, against the attempt of foreign or homebred enemies.

"4. That he hath rebelliously and mutinously said, that if Thos. Gerrard, Esq. (of the council), did not come and bring his wife and children to his church, he would come and force them to the church, contrary to a known Act of Assembly in this province.

"Rt. Honourable—Since I writ my last to you, I have received a message from Mrs. Gerrard, which is that Mr. Fitzherbert hath threatened excommunication to Mr. Gerrard, because he doth not bring to his church his wife and children. And further, Mr. Fitzherbert saith, that he hath written home to ye head of the Church in England, and that if it be their judgments to have it so he will come with a party and compel them. My lord, this I offer to your lordship, as Mrs. Gerrard's relation, who I think would not offer to report any such thing if it were not so. And, my lord, I thank God, ye government of ye country is now in your officers' hands. But I think (and I have good grounds to think so) that it will not long continue there if such things be not remedied. I told Mr. Fitzherbert of it, about a year since in private, and also that such things were against the law of ye country. Yet his answer was, that he must be

well as the desecration of the *most holy* institutions; the latter defining or bounding the pledge of religious freedom to the Roman Catholic by securing the same liberty for the English churchman. And there cannot be reasonable doubt, that among statesmen as well as ecclesiastics, two centuries ago, the Lord's Day and the Trinity (or funda-

directed by his conscience more than by the law of any country. I do not, my lord, thrust myself upon any business of quarrel; but it is peace and quietness I desire. And I hope your lordship hath no other cause but to wish the same. And so I refer the consideration of it to you; and remain your lordship's most faithful servant to command,—HEN: COURSEY.

"Thos. Gerrard, Esq., saith upon oath, that having conference with Mr. Fitzherbert, as they were walking in the woods, and in his own orchard, touching ye bringing his children to the Roman Catholic Church, he gave Mr. Fitzherbert reasons why it was not safe for himself and this deponent. And the said Mr. Fitzherbert told his deponent that he would compel and force them, And likewise, he said, that he would excommunicate him; for he would make him know that he had to do with ye bringing up of his children and his estate.

"The deposition of Robt. Slye, aged 30 years, or thereabouts, sworn and examined in open court, saith:—That some time in or about July or August in the year 1656, Mr. Fitzherbert being then at this deponent's house, this deponent desired Mr. Fitzherbert to inform him who it was that had scandalously and falsely accused him of beating his Irish servants, because they refused to be of the same religion of him, the said deponent. Which request Mr. Fitzherbert refused to grant, saying that he did believe the report to be false; and therefore desired him, this deponent, not further to urge him in that business, for he would not, and could not, disclose the author thereof. Mr. Fitzherbert told ye said deponent that Mr. Gerrard had also beaten an Irish servant of his likewise, because she refused to be a Protestant, or go to prayer with those of his

mental article of revealed religion) were two of the "*most sacred*" things of God. This fact accounts for the penalty against those who were guilty of violating the sanctity of the "Sabbath;" or of "cursing" God, that is denying the great doctrine of the Athanasian creed.

2. A history is not an argument. In any other

family that were so. To which the said deponent replied, that that story was *like the other* (or words to yt purpose); from which discourse likewise we fell to other relating to Mr. Gerrard and the children. Mr. Fitzherbert told him, the said deponent, that Mr. Gerrard, although he professed himself a Roman Catholic, yet his life and conversation was not agreeable to his profession. The said deponent asked him his reason. Mr. Fitzherbert answered, because he brought not his wife and children to the Roman Catholic Church. Moreover, he told him, the said deponent, that if Mr. Gerrard would not bring his children to his church he would force and compel him thereunto, if he were the same in reality, that he pretended himself to be. Moreover, that if Mr. Gerrard's life and conversation was not otherwise for the future than what it had been formerly, he would draw his sword against him, if he made choice of him for his father confessor, or to that effect. By the word *sword* this deponent understood, that he meant the censure of ye church. But this deponent understood not what he meant by the words *force* or *compel*. Mr. Fitzherbert told this deponent further, that if Mr. Gerrard brought not his children freely to his church, nor educated them in the principles of the Romish religion, he would take such a course that he would undertake their education in Mr. Gerrard's own house, whether Mr. Gerrard would give way thereunto or no. This deponent advised Mr. Fitzherbert to forbear to proceed according to such resolution. Whereupon, after long arguing about this business, Mr. Fitzherbert told the said deponent that if he would tell him his opinion, what it were best to do in relation to Mr. Gerrard, his wife, and children; and he, the said Mr. Fitzher-

place, a dispute indeed upon a question of religious decency would be quite as useless as one upon a point of taste. But the world, either Roman Catholic or Protestant, is hardly yet so wise as to be prepared to condemn Lord Baltimore and the Assembly of Maryland for the imposition of a fine of five pounds upon the man who should dare to

bert, promised him to follow his counsel. This deponent advised him not to disturb Mrs. Gerrard nor her children, in relation to their religion, or words to yt effect, as the deponent hath declared. And further saith not.

"Henry Keine, sworn in open court, maketh oath, that he went to Mrs. Brooke's house upon a summons to a muster, the 24th of July last, when Mr. Fitzherbert made a sermon. And Mr. Fitzherbert, coming forth, demanded of them how they liked his doctrine. And further, ye said Mr. Fitzherbert said, if any would give him leave to be in their house, he would now and then come and give them a sermon. And, if he could get leave of the governor, he would preach at the court-house. That night, or the next day, Richard Games, turning Catholic, came home, and brought two books with him, which he said Mr. Fitzherbert gave him. And further saith not.

"John Grammer maketh oath, that he was present at the muster at Mrs. Brooke's house, at the same time. And there he heard a declaration, or sermon, by Mr. Fitzherbert, not expecting any. And after sermon Mr. Fitzherbert said, that if the people in this river would hear him he would come now and then and give them a sermon. He asked them how they liked his doctrine. But he heard nobody make answer to him. The next day being Sunday, this deponent and his wife, going to Mrs. Brooke, he met there Mr. Fitzherbert, who asked him again how he liked his sermon. Who answered, yt some things he liked, and other some he did not like. Mr. Fitzherbert then asked him what those things were he did not like? and walked out with this deponent, when they had a quarter of an hour's discourse. And in discourse, he gave him, this

speak reproachfully of "The Blessed Virgin," or of the heroic evangelists and apostolic martyrs of the primitive church.

3. There is a striking difference between religious uniformity and social harmony. And it was an object of the law to tolerate the want of the one, and to promote the growth of the other. In this particular, it was but the development of the policy which had been adopted under the first governor's administration. Bounded by the preceding explanations, the law throughout breathes the spirit of peace and charity as well as harmony.

4. Freedom, in the fullest sense, was secured to all believers in Christianity; to Roman Catholics and Protestants; to Episcopalians and Puritans; to Calvinists and Arminians; and to Christians of

deponent, indifferent good satisfaction—his memory being but weak on Scripture. And in conclusion of the discourse, Captain Thos. Brooke came and called ye said Mr. Fitzherbert in to dinner. And (whether after dinner or before he remembereth not) he gave him a little catechism book, desiring him to read it; bidding him, after he had read yt book, call to Richard Games for another book. And further saith not." See Lib. S. 1658 to 1662. Judgments pp. 102–105.

On page 1082 is the following:—

"Then was put an information against Francis Fitzherbert, by his Lordship's attorney-general, folio 102.

every other name coming within the meaning of the Assembly. A Christian was a believer in Jesus Christ. The belief in Christ was synonymous with a faith in his divinity. And the recognition of his God-head, was equivalent (such is the clear intention of the Act) to a confession of that article in the apostolic creed, which teaches the great doctrine of the Trinity. The act of the Assembly also fully explains the oath which had been imposed upon the governor, and the privy counsellors. And the believer enjoyed not only a freedom but also a protection. He who "troubled, molested, or discountenanced" him, was, according to the law, fined for his offence.

5. From the language of the Act, as well as the subsequent practice of the government, it is evi-

"To which Francis Fitzherbert demurred in law:

"1. Neither denying or confessing the matter here objected, since by the very first law of this country, Holy Church, within this province, shall have and enjoy all her rights, liberties, and franchises, wholly and without blemish, amongst which that of preaching and teaching is not the least. Neither imports it what church is there meant; since, by the true intent of the Act concerning religion, every church professing to believe in God the Father, Son, and Holy Ghost, is accounted Holy Church here.

"2. Because, by the act entitled An Act Concerning Religion, it is provided that no person whatsoever professing to believe in Jesus Christ shall be molested

dent that the quiet disbeliever also was protected. A case can easily be given. But it is enough for the reader to look at that section of the law, which forbids the application, in a reproachful sense, to "any person or persons whatsoever," of any "name or term" "relating to matter of religion."

The Act, it will be observed, covers a very broad ground. It is true, it did not embrace every class of subsequent religionists. A Jew, without peril to his life, could not call the Saviour of the world a "magician," or a "necromancer. A Quaker, under the order of the government, was required to take off his hat in court, or go immediately to the whipping-post. The Mormon, who dignifies polygamy with the notion of a sacrament, who disseminates the gospel in the propagation of his

for or in respect of his or her religion, or the free exercise thereof. And undoubtedly preaching and teaching is the free exercise of every churchman's religion. And upon this I crave judgment.

"To the first and second point in the information put against the said Francis Fitzherbert the' demurrer is allowed. The third point depends upon the two first, and is dis-allowed.

"The opinion of the Board is, that it is neither rebellion nor mutiny to utter such words as alleged in the 4th article, if it were proved." See Lib. S. 1658 to 1662, Judgments, p. 1082.

species, would not have been allowed, we may suppose, to marry more than one woman. But as early as 1659, a well-known non-believer in the Trinity lived here, transacted his business, and instituted without objection his suits in the civil courts; nor were the Jewish disabilities entirely removed, till a period long after the American Revolution; and this feature of the law, all things considered, was not more of a reproach to the legislators of 1649 than the constitution of the State to the reformers of 1774. We have no evidence, indeed, that any Quakers were in Maryland, at the passage of the law; and when they came, their case was misunderstood; for the dislike toward them arose from their supposed want of respect for the constituted authorities, and their refusal to take the oath of submission. A constitutional difficulty might also readily occur to any one, as it certainly did to the proprietary, who was bound by the charter to maintain the fundamental principles of Anglo-Saxon law, which had always regarded the instrumentality of the oath in the administration of practical justice, as the corner-stone of a system. But every disposition was manifested to render them comfortable. And they soon became a flourishing and influential denomination. Notwithstanding the imperfection which ever marks human legislation, it is wonderful to think how far our ancestors went in the march of religious freedom. The earliest policy of Maryland was in striking contrast with that of every other colony. The toleration, which prevailed from the first, and fifteen years later was formally ratified by the voice of the people, must, therefore, be regarded as the living embodiment of a great idea; the introduction of a new element into the civilization of Anglo-American humanity; the beginning of another movement in the progress of the human mind.[1]

[1] Toleration, in the widest sense, or in the most strictly logical acceptation, exists only in a State founded upon naked atheism. The history of the whole of Western Christendom (I speak of Europe), for a period of many centuries, exhibits but the perpetual struggle between the Church and the State, arising from the sometimes quiet, but always uniform tendency of the one to absorb the other. The conflict is illustrated in the most striking manner, by glancing at the jurisdiction constantly claimed and denied over the important institution of marriage. The interesting case of the

Rev. Wm. Wilkinson (for Mormonism I am unwilling to touch), will be given from our records, in a further part of this volume.

With regard to the Quakers, it may be proper to add, that, while I do not assert there never was a practical case of whipping, I can sincerely say I have never met with any. I am clearly of the opinion that some of our writers have indulged in very great exaggeration. As early as Fox's visit, many Quakers were here. The speaker of the Assembly attended his meeting. Judges of the county courts, wives of privy counsellors, and a large number of the most prominent colonists became his disciples. The general spirit of the proprietary's government cannot be mistaken. No principle in history is better settled. And I cannot, therefore, so easily or readily regard the case of the Quakers in the light of a practical anomaly. See Fox's Journal—a very interesting book—and the next chapter of this volume.

In the text, I have referred to Dr. Lumbrozo, the well-known Jew (for he seems to have observed no secrecy), who lived some time in Maryland, without rebuke from the government, in the usual exercise of his calling, and of the right to institute actions in the Civil Court. We cannot doubt he was also allowed the *quiet* enjoyment of his religion. But he was accused of blasphemy; and although he fortunately escaped a trial, in consequence of the pardon accompanying the proclamation in favor of Richard, the son of the lord protector—a proclamation which was issued but a few days after the accusation—the case is one which was instituted under the Act of 1649; and I, therefore, give the proceeding as it occurs upon the Records of the Provincial Court, Lib. S. 1658 to 1662, Judgments, pp. 159–160.

"At a Provincial Court, held at St. Mary's on Wednesday, this 23d February, 1658.

"Present—Josias Fendall, Esq., Governor; Philip Calvert, Esq., Secretary; Mr. Robert Clarke; Mr. Baker Brooke; Dr. Luke Barber.

"Was called afore the Board, Jacob Lumbrozo, and charged by his Lordship's Attorney for uttering words of blasphemy against our Blessed Saviour, Jesus Christ.

"The deposition of John Hoffsett, aged 44 years, or thereabouts, sayeth this 19th day of February, 1658:—

"That, about half a year since, this deponent being at ye house of Mr. Richard Preston, and there meeting with Jacob Lumbrozo, he, this deponent, and the said Lumbrozo falling into discourse concerning our Blessed Saviour, Christ, his resurrection, telling ye said Lumbrozo that he was more than man, as did appear by his resurrection. To which the said Lumbrozo answered, that his disciples stole him away. Then this deponent replied, yt no man ever did such miracles as he. To which ye said Lumbrozo answered, that such works might be done by necromancy or sorcery, or words to that purpose. And this deponent replied to ye said Lumbrozo, yt he supposed yt ye said Lumbrozo took Christ to be a necromancer. To which ye said Lumbrozo answered nothing, but laughed. And further this deponent sayeth not.

"Jurat die et anno supradict. cor. me,

"Henry Coursey.

"I, Richard Preston, jr., do testify yt, about June or July last past, coming from Thomas Thomas's, in company with Josias Cole and ye Jew Doctor, known by ye name of Jacob Lumbrozo, the said Josias Cole asked ye said Lumbrozo, whether ye Jews did look for a Messias? And ye said Lumbrozo answered, yes. Then ye said Cole asked him, what He was that was crucified at Jerusalem? And ye said Lumbrozo answered, He was a man. Then ye said Cole asked him, how He did do all His miracles? And ye said Lumbrozo answered, He did them by ye Art Magic. Then ye said Cole asked him, how His disciples did do ye same miracles, after He was crucified? And ye said Lumbrozo answered, that He taught them His art. And further saith not.

"This was declared before me, as in the presence of God, that it is true, this 21st of February, 1658. HENRY COURSEY.

"The said Lumbrozo saith, that he had some talk with those persons, and willed by them to declare his opinion, and by his profession, a Jew, he answered to some particular demands then urged. And as to that of miracles done by art magic, he declared what remains written concerning Moses and ye Magicians of Egypt. But said not anything scoffingly, or in derogation of Him Christians acknowledge for their Messias.

"It is ordered, that ye said Lumbrozo remain in ye Sheriff's custody, until he put in security, body for body, to make answer to what shall be laid to his charge concerning those blasphemous words and speeches, at ye next Provincial Court; and yt the persons be then present to testify, *viva voce*, in Court.

"*Mittimus.*—To ye Sheriff of St. Mary's County, according to the order *Supradict.*"

N.B.—The reader will observe, that Ri. Preston, a Quaker, simply declares.

CHAPTER VIII.

The influence of the Legislation of 1649 upon the Colonization of Maryland—Arrival of Families—Foundation of Settlements. Erection of Counties.

THE liberal policy of Maryland could not fail to attract the attention of the other Anglo-American colonies. The Puritans upon the James and upon the Elizabeth, having, in consequence of their *non-conformity*, been ordered to leave Virginia, soon found an asylum here, and during the latter part of 1649, and the beginning of 1650, founded (under the patronage, it is supposed, of Governor Stone) several settlements at Greenberry's Point, and upon the Severn[1]—the whole body consisting of

[1] It is generally believed that the first settlement of the Puritans was at the point where the city of Annapolis stands; and that the foundation of that city was laid almost immediately after their arrival. I can only say, there is no recorded evidence within my knowledge, of the facts. The earliest settlement which I can discover (the one of 1649) was at Greenberry's Point, a

more than one hundred persons, distinguished not less for their intelligence than for the fervor of their religious feelings, and for the stubbornness of their wills—destined, also, at no distant period, to take a very conspicuous part in the affairs of the province. One of them was the ancestor of the extinct Bennetts of Bennett's Point in Queen Anne's;[1] the descent of the Lloyds of Wye House, is derived from a second;[2] and a third was the

peninsula of the Chesapeake, a little below the mouth of the Severn. My belief is, that Annapolis was not founded till many years later. But at Greenberry's Point a town was laid out the very first year of the settlement there; and the tract running down to the point, and now in the possession of Capt. Taylor, was originally called Town Neck, as the history of the land-title will clearly show. See also my Historical Letter in the summer of 1854, to Mr. Ch. Justice Le Grand, upon the files of the Baltimore *American*, of the New York *Churchman*, and, if I mistake not, of other newspapers.

[1] Richard, whose tombstone is still preserved at Bennett's Point, the largest landholder of the province, and to whom tradition has uniformly given the prefix of "Squire," was the grandson of the Richard, who, soon after the settlement at Greenberry's Point, returned to Virginia, and became the governor of that colony.

[2] Edward, who came from Virginia, was many years a privy councillor of Maryland, but died at an advanced age, in the city of London. James, a descendant of the privy councillor, was the

progenitor of the Marshes of Kent Island, now represented,[1] through a female line, by the Formans of Rose Hill and of Clover Fields, and by several other distinguished families of the Eastern shore. Two of them, James Cox and George Puddington, represented Anne Arundel at St. Mary's, in the legislature of 1650; the former being elected the speaker of that assembly. And they both signed the celebrated Declaration setting forth the "fitting and convenient freedom" which Protestants enjoyed, in the "exercise," of their religion, under the government of the Roman Catholic proprietary.[2] The name of the Puritan speaker is the very first upon the list of signers.

ancestor of the family of Nichols, now residing at Derby, in Kent county. The Tilghmans also are descendants, through another female line, of the Hon. Edw. Lloyd, the emigrant.

[1] Capt. Marsh, of Kent Island, with a residence also at Chestertown, and the fourth in the direct line from the Hon. Thomas Marsh inclusive, died, at an advanced age, during the early stage of the American Revolution. Each generation was represented by one gentleman only; and they all bore the name of Thomas, still perpetuated in the Rose Hill branch. The captain was the last of the male line The first Thomas held a seat in the council.

[2] In Langford's "Refutation" of Leonard Strong's "Babylon's

The settlement also upon South River was an interesting one. It was founded in 1650; and consisted chiefly of Puritans of a milder type than

Fall," and in Bozman's Maryland (see vol. 2, pp. 672–673), we have this important document.

DECLARATION.

"The declaration and certificate of William Stone, Esquire, lieutenant of the Province of Maryland, by commission from the right honorable the Lord Baltimore, Lord Proprietary thereof, and of Captain John Price, Mr. Thomas Hatton, and Captain Robert Vaughan, of his said Lordship's Council there, and of divers of the Burgesses now met in the Assembly there, and other *Protestant* inhabitants of the said Province, made the 17th day of April, Anno Dom., one thousand, six hundred and fifty.

"We the said Lieutenant, Council, Burgesses, and other *Protestant* inhabitants above mentioned, whose names are hereunto subscribed, do declare and certify to all persons whom it may concern, That, according to an act of Assembly here, and several other strict injunctions and declarations by his said Lordship for that purpose made and provided, we do here enjoy all fitting and convenient freedom and liberty in the exercise of our religion, under his Lordship's government and interest; And that none of us are anyways troubled or molested, for or by reason thereof, within his Lordship's said province.

William Stone, *Governor*.

Jo. Price,
Robert Vaughan,
Tho. Hatton, } *Council.*

James Cox,
Tho. Steerman,
John Hatche,
George Puddington,
Robert Robines,
Walter Bain,
William Brough,
Francis Poesy. } *Burgesses.*

*William Durand
Anthony Rawlins
Thomas Maydwell

Note.—That James Cox and George Puddington were then Burgesses for the people at Ann Arundell.

* *Note.*—That this is the same man who attests Mr. Strong's pamphlet before mentioned.

those upon the Severn, and of Anglo-Catholics from England. One of the most prominent colonists upon this river was the Hon. Wm. Burgess, who bore the arms [1] of the family at Truro, in Cornwall (*or, a fesse chequy, or and gules, in chief three crosses-crosslet-fitcheé of the last*), but sustained a very near relationship to the Burgesses of Marlborough in Wilts, and whose daughter was the

Marke Bloomfield	Elias Beech
Thomas Bushell	George Sawyer
William Hungerford	William Edis
William Stumpson	John Gage
Thomas Dinyard	Robert Ward
John Grinsdith	William Marshall
William Edwin	Richard Smith
Richard Browne	Arthur Turner
William Pell	William Hawley
William Warren	William Smoot
Edward Williams	John Sturman
Raph Beane	John Nichols
John Slingsby	Hugh Crage
James Morphen	George Whitacre
Francis Martin	Daniel Clocker
John Walker	John Perin
Stanhop Roberts	Patrick Forrest
William Browne	George Beckwith
John Halfehead	Thomas Warr
William Hardwick	Walter Waterling."

[1] An impression from his seal is still preserved.

wife of Lord Chas. Baltimore's step-son. About 1680, he founded the once little flourishing, but now extinct, town of London. From this town's successful rivalship with Annapolis, during the first few years; from the antiquity of the South River Club (the oldest probably on the continent); and from the superior style of the monumental inscriptions at the parish church and upon the plantations; I infer, the settlement, in point of intellectual culture and refinement, upon this river, was in advance of the one upon the other. Of all the provincial governors, whose tombstones are preserved, or I have been fortunate enough, at least, to find, Col. Burgess is the one whose epitaph is the oldest [1]

[1] EPITAPH.

Here lyeth ye body of W. Burges,
Esq., who departed this life on ye
24 day of Janu., 1686;
Aged about 64 years; leaving his
Dear beloved wife Ursula, and eleven
Children; viz. seven sons and four daughters,
And eight grand children.
In his life-time, he was a Member of
His Lordship's Council of State; one

Twenty miles from the mouth of the Patuxent, during the same year (1650), a Protestant settlement (probably Anglo-Catholic) was founded by Robert Brooke, from England; consisting originally of forty persons—their names are still preserved[1]—

Of his Lordship's Deputy-Governors;
A Justice of ye High Provincial Court;
Colon. of a regiment of ye Trained Bands;
And sometimes General of all ye
Military Forces of this Province.
His loving wife Ursula, his Executrix,
In testimony of her true respect,
And due regard to the worthy
Deserts of her dear deceased
Husband, hath erected this Monument.

[1] "The names of people come out of England, and arrived in Maryland, June 30, 1650, at the cost and charge of Robert Brooke, Esq.

Robt. Brooke	Thomas Brooke	John Brook.
Mary his wife;	Charles Brooke	Wm. Brooke
His children	Roger Brooke	Francis Brooke
Baker Brooke	Robt. Brooke	Mary Brooke
		Anna Brooke.

MEN-SERVANTS.

Marke Lovely	Wm. Bradney	Rich. Robinson.
Marke King	Phil. Harwood	Anthony Kitchin

and including his own very large family, now represented by the Brookes of Brooke-Grove in Montgomery, and by a vast number of descendants in Prince George's, and in other counties of the western shore. One of his representatives, through a female line, is Roger Brooke Taney, the present chief justice of the United States. The settlement was erected into a county, under the name of Charles; and one of Mr. Brooke's sons created lord of the manor,[1] which formed the chief seat of the little colony. Under a commission from the proprietary, Mr. Brooke was the first commander of the county. He also held a seat in the

Wm. Jones	Thos. Joyce	Robt. Hooper
John Clifford	Henry Peere	Wm. Hinson
James Leigh	Thomas Elstone	John Boocock
Benjamin Hammond	Edward Cooke	David Brown
Robt. Sheale	Ambrose Briggs	Henry Robinson.

MAID-SERVANTS.

Anne Marshall	Abigael Mountague
Katherine Fisher	Eleanor Williams
Elizabeth Williamson	Agnes Neale
Margarite Watts.	Forty persons.

LAND RECORDS, Lib. No. I. pp. 165, 166.

[1] The name of the manor was *De la Brooke.*

privy council; and, at a little later period, but during the ascendency of the Puritans, was elevated to the post of president—an office analogous to that of lieutenant-general, or governor.

The mild and gentle Friend also came—unkindly treated, it is said, at first—the reasons have been suggested—but in due course of time, much better understood, and saving a single exception (the one relating to the oath[1]), made joyful and happy, in a religious and in every other particular. Fox, himself, appeared—the chief of the Quakers—a great reformer—a man of rude, but powerful eloquence, and whose fame had preceded his mission to the New World—travelling with an energy almost incredible over various parts of the continent, through forests and thickets, through deep marshes and dangerous bogs—crossing rivers and bays in canoes—and sleeping in the open woods by a fire—preaching at the cliffs of the Patuxent, and upon the banks of the Severn, upon the Choptank and

[1] Even from the statements and few extracts in Ridgely's excellent Annals, it is quite evident, that the constitutional question (ante, p. 63) was mooted, at an early day.

elsewhere, to Indians and crowds of colonists[1]—speaking before aboriginal kings, and leading emigrants from the old world—giving utterance to the Spirit, in words of fire and with all the apparent life of an apostle—thus promoting the growth of a denomination which soon absorbed a large number of the Puritans,[2] and embraced many of the most respectable and some of the most distinguished families of the province. In 1672, exclusive of Fox, there were at least seven ministers of the Society of Friends in Maryland! The names are all of them still known.[3]

[1] Fox's "Journal."

[2] The cliffs of Calvert, the banks of West River, and the Choptank, were, it seems, the early rallying-points of this denomination. And while some of the Puritans sympathized with Episcopacy, a large number embraced the faith of the great preacher. The Prestons, the Sharpes, the Thomases, and many others, might be cited. The Richardsons also of West River—originally, it is supposed, of the Puritan type—became prominent Quakers; and the prevalence of Fox's doctrines is evident from the preservation of the wills (to omit other proof) containing contributions to the fund for the support of the body, and bearing the strongly-marked phraseology, for which the Friends have always been noted.

[3] An island of the Chesapeake, near the mouth of the Choptank perpetuates the name of a well-known Quaker. It was originally

Flying from discontent, from turmoil, and misery, some of the Swedes[1] and of the Dutch,

called Clayborne's. For there the founder of the Kent Island colony, we may presume, established a trading-post, like the one upon Palmer's, now Watson's; or perhaps planted a small settlement, as he also did, as early as 1636, through the agency of his "cousin," Ri. Thompson, upon Poplar, still nearer Kent Island. But Sharpe's Island was held by Doct. Peter Sharpe, for some time before 1672, or the year of Fox's appearance. "I give," says the Doctor (see his will of 1672, Lib. No. 1, 1635 to 1674, p. 496), "to Friends in ye ministry, viz. Alice Gary, William Cole, and Sarah Mash" (intended doubtless for Mrs. *Marsh*, the widow of the Hon. Thos. Marsh), "if then in being; Winlock Christeson and his wife; John Burnett, and Daniel Gould; in money or goods, at the choice of my executors, forty shillings' worth apiece; also for a perpetual standing, a horse, for the use of Friends in ye ministry, and to be placed at the convenient place for their use." There is also other evidence in the will, that Doct. Sharpe was a Friend. But writers as respectable as Kilty (see "Land-holder's-Assistant," p. 88) are so horror-struck at the "indignities" with which the "strangers" were treated, that they do not even admit the probability, that the testator of 1672 was a disciple of Fox. Nor are they in the least aware of the early and extensive spread of the Quakers in Maryland.

[1] The settlement and subsequent fate of the Swedes suggest a subject for one of the saddest, yet sweetest chapters, in the history of American colonization. Planted upon the Delaware, under the auspices of a crown distinguished for its noble qualities; but overlaid, if not crushed, in the infancy of the colony, by the supe-

who had founded the respective settlements upon the Delaware, received a glad and joyful welcome.

rior numbers, first of the Dutch, and then of the English; they still retained, in the midst of all their reverses, the fond remembrance of their native land; and cherished, with a gentle but glowing love, the faith and traditions of their original ancestry. Eight generations also have lingered around the gravestone and the hearth of their early American forefathers; nor have they yet lost those elements so characteristic of their race, and which, in spite of so much that is mean in every age, have imparted such real dignity to human nature. But some of them wandered off, at the period of their severest sufferings, and three were upon Kent Island about 1665. There also did Valerius Leo and Andrew Hanson find their early grave. The heart of Major Joseph Wickes was touched at the lonely condition of Hanse, the orphan of Mr. Hanson; and to the young Swede he was, it seems, a father. The child became a man. He rose to a high official rank, and held the most honorable posts in Kent County. Upon the seal of Col. Hanse Hanson's near descendant, is preserved a coat of arms, consisting of four lilies, with something strongly resembling a cross; and there are representatives of his family now living in Maryland. One of his descendants was the late Mrs. Doct. Wroth, of Chestertown.

The number of the Dutch refugees was larger than that of the Swedish; including the governor, Alexander Diniossa, and his children, originally from Gilderland. He lived sometime upon an island of the Chesapeake, then called "Foster's;" but subsequently, it seems, upon the western shore. And the last glimpse I obtain is in Prince George's county, where his family dwindled

They lived and died among us. Their blood, for many generations, has been mingled with that of the other colonists. And from them have sprung some of the most patriotic sons of Maryland.

In 1660, a small colony from the mouth of the Hudson was founded upon the Bohemia River, by Augustine Herman, a very remarkable man.[1] A manor also of the same name, still a well-known locality, was erected in consideration of the highly meritorious services[2] he had rendered the proprietary. And he has descendants through various female lines who now do honor to the State.

down into a state either of extreme misfortune or of great obscurity.

[1] Honorably connected with the early diplomatic histories both of New York and of Maryland. See Albany Records; and his embassy to Maryland, Bancroft. See also Brodhead. It is due to the memory of Herman to add, that he derived a title to the land upon the Bohemia, not only from the proprietary, a sufficient security, but also from the Indians. The consideration is given in one of his journals preserved in the Land Office, at Annapolis. A copy is also in the possession of Col. Spencer's family.

[2] The preparation of a map of Maryland and Virginia—a work, at that time, of great labor—and the best, in the opinion of the English Crown, which had appeared—but a great curiosity, no doubt, at present—and a good illustration of the imperfect state

The tidings went also to the Old World. Gladdened with the prospect of religious liberty, and invited by a policy so liberal in all other respects, strangers arrived from England[1] and from Wales;[2]

of geographical knowledge at the date of its publication. I have never seen it; but presume it is still extant.

I have been informed that the Oldhams, the Bayards, the Maclanes, and other families, claim a descent from the proud Bohemian. But the only ones coming within the proof to which I have had access are those of Thompson, Forman, Chambers, Spencer, and their various branches. Within, or near the Manor, was a small community, which held the principles of Labady; including the one which abolishes private property, by a surrender of every thing to the common stock. One of Herman's sons embraced the faith of that visionary French divine—a source of real grief to the lord of the manor during his latter years—and the occasion which demanded a codicil, in which he tied up the title to his large possessions.

[1] In Appendix, No. 1, I shall notice the arrival of the families of Burgess, Ringgold, Hynson, Dunn, Wickes, Leeds, Stone, Carroll, Paca, Chase, Pearce, Pratt, Chambers, Goldsborough, Tilghman, Hawkins, Thompson, Wroth, Sewall, Sprigg, Taney, Tyler, Lowe, Claggett, Addison, Dorsey, and of Darnall. Most of them were Protestants. They furnish some of the best representatives of the early provincial gentry of Maryland. And they nearly all held some post of honor, under the dominion of the first and of the second proprietary.

[2] The Lloyds, the Thomases, the Snowdens, the Richardsons, the

from Scotland[1] and from Ireland; from the dominions of the kings of France and of Spain; from

Shipleys, and many other families, came, it is supposed, from the Principality. The Severn and the Wye, upon which the Hon. Edward Lloyd resided, were no doubt named after the rivers of Wales, in honor of his native land.

The Thomases, it is said, first lived upon Kent Island; but according to the earliest recorded information I have been able to obtain, they resided in Anne Arundel, near Thomas's Point, about 1655. Philip, the emigrant, was a privy councillor, and many of his descendants held high public positions, including Phil. Evan Thomas, now living at a very advanced age, the projector and first president of the Baltimore & Ohio Railroad. Upon a gold-headed cane, handed down from an early generation, I have seen the arms borne by a well-known family of Wales, a branch of which once existed near Swansea and Bristol.

The Snowdens arrived about 1660. They were the ancestors of the large family living in Prince George's and in other counties.

The Richardsons resided many generations upon West River. They came, probably, about 1665. There is a branch at Eutaw-Place, near the Monocacy.

The Shipleys, a family of planters in Anne Arundel, and subsequently in several other counties, arrived, I am inclined to think, at a period but little later. One branch of this family is at Enfield Chase.

[1] The settlement, near the site of Washington city, long before the erection of Prince George's, but which subsequently formed a hundred of that county, bore the name of *New Scotland.*

the States of Holland, and from various parts of Germany; from Sweed-land, the country of the

And two of the largest families of Maryland—the Magruders and the Beales—undoubtedly came from Scotland. So, also, it seems, did the Bowies, the Edmonstones, and other families. The Magruders arrived about 1655. One of their earliest seats was upon the western branch of the Patuxent. Alexander, the emigrant, died about 1680, leaving his children, Alexander, Nathaniel, James, John, Samuel, and Elizabeth. The Beales, I think, came some time after the Magruders. Col. Ninian Beale is the earliest I remember. The Bowies (ancestors of the governor) and the Edmonstones, did not arrive, it would appear, before the Protestant Revolution. Archibald, the progenitor of the latter, is the first representative of whom I have any knowledge; and a relation, it is supposed, to the family of Sir Archibald Edmonstone, of Scotland. He was the progenitor of the Edmonstones, near Bladensburg, one of whom was a leading provincial judge of Prince George's County Court; and the ancestor, through a female line, of the Lachlans of Montgomery, but now in the State of Missouri; and of the wife and children of Gov. Hempstead, of Iowa.

A few only of a high social rank arrived from Ireland. I remember no prominent ones, excepting the De Courcys, who, it is supposed, emigrated from that country. Cheston, their present family seat, has been held for a period of nearly two hundred years. It is difficult to say, with certainty, at what time, or from what country, the Worthingtons came. John, of Anne Arundel County, who died about 1700, and who, it appears, was the first of the Maryland line, gave his home planta-

great Gustavus, the champion of Protestant christendom; and from the very heart of the kingdom of Bohemia, the land of Jerome and of Huss.

The pious emigrant of every name, who believed

tion upon the Severn, to his son, John; "Greenberry's Forest" to Thomas; and to William, "Howard's Inheritance," with two other tracts, the one near "Mr. Richard Beard's Mill," the other at "The Fresh Pond, in the Bodkin Creek of Patapsco River."

The Causins, of Causin's Manor; the Jarbos, of St. Mary's; the Lamars, of Prince George's and other counties (one of whom was a gallant officer of the American revolutionary army); the Du Valles, of Anne Arundel, ancestors of a judge of the United States Supreme Court; the Brashaers, of Anne Arundel and of Prince George's, represented also by the late Doct. Brashaer, of New Market, Frederick county; and the Lacounts, of the eastern shore, ancestors of the chief justice of Kansas; are some of our oldest French families. There is also but little doubt that the Ricauds of Kent, represented by the Hon. Jas. B. Ricaud, came also, originally, if not directly, from France. Colonel Jarbo, and the ancestor of the Hon Jno. M. S. Causin, arrived before the year 1649; the Ricauds, about 1650; and the Brashaers (directly from Virginia) at a period not much later. They all arrived before the Protestant Revolution of 1689. There is the strongest presumption that the Contees (about the time of their arrival closely connected with the family of Gov. Seymour, and lately represented by the gallant John Contee, of Java) came also, originally, from France; though there is evidence of the fact, that they had lived at Barnstaple, in Devonshire, as did some of the most distinguished

only in CHRIST, could securely sit under his own vine or bower, or still more unpretending roof; and the weeping penitent at his rude altar or humble hearth-stone, might offer up his confession and his prayer. To the children of sorrow and to the victims of persecution, to men of various races, of divers languages, and of many religions, the voice

Huguenots in other parts of England before their emigration to other countries. The arrival, however, of the Contees in Maryland was late. I doubt if it was before the year 1690.

Four of Capt. James Neal's children were born within the Spanish or Portuguese dominions, and subsequently naturalized by an Act of our Assembly. So also were Anthony Brispoe, Barbara de Barette, and probably other emigrants. See Liber, "Laws, C. & W. H., 1638 to 1678."

A large number came from Holland and Germany, including the families of "Comegyes" and Lockerman. See last-named liber, where also I have obtained the birth-place of many alien emigrants.

Axell Still, John Elexon, Oliver Colke, Marcus Syserson, Jeffrey Jacobson, Mounts Anderson, Cornelius Peterson, and Andrew Clements, may be named among those who were born in Sweden.

Augustine Herman, the founder and original lord of Bohemia Manor, was born at the city of Prague. Manhattan, now New York, was the birth-place of most of his children. See Liber, "Laws, C. & W. H., 1638 to 1678," p. 158. His wife also was probably born at Prague.

of our early legislators was like the "sound" from a better world—like a second evangely from the skies! For they spoke, "every" one in his "own tongue," "the wonderful works of God."

I have attempted to trace the birth and early growth of our religious liberty, under its successive phases; showing the harmony between the proprietary and the planters; explaining the legislation of the provincial Assembly according to the rights and obligations springing out of the charter; and sketching the effects of so liberal a system upon the colonization of Maryland. Without reference to the credit due either to the Roman Catholic or to the Protestant Assemblymen of 1649, it is but proper to add, what will be denied by no one at all familiar with the colonial records, that the legislative policy so honorable to our ancestors and so beneficial in its influence, underwent no material change, except a few years later, at the short period of the ascendency of the Puritans; and in 1689, at the complete overthrow of the proprietary's government—an event which resulted in the establishment of the Anglican church, and in the persecution of the Roman Catholics.

The history of the Protestant revolution in 1689 has never yet been fully written. But there is evidence upon the records of the English government to show it was the result of a panic, produced by one of the most dishonorable falsehoods[1] which

[1] The following documents are taken from the English State Paper Office. As specimens of the spelling, of the method of abbreviation, and of the punctuation, nearly two hundred years ago, the first five are printed in a style which resembles the copies sent me:

REPORT OF COMMISSIONERS TO THE INDIANS.

23 AUGUST, 1689.

S. P. O.
B. T. Maryland,
Vol. 1, *B. D.* 25½.

August ye 23d, '89.

These may acquaint yo^{w}, that we whose names are underwritten have, according to request, bin and treated with ye Indians, and doe find 'em to be very civill and kind, and desire nothing butt peace and quiettness, butt y^{t} in part thorough ye instigation of bad people, and chiefly doe instance Andrew Gray, that ye English in one moone would cutt them all of; likewise, concerning an Indian woman, wch they say was kill'd by Cornelius Mulraine's wife, wch they have expected some satisfactory answer, concerning which as yett they have not received. Also, y^{t} ye s^{d} Cornelius since their departure offer'd great abuse in robbing them of their cannous, corn, matts, bowles, and basketts, and they say their chests have been broke open, and since they have bin gone out, ye s^{d} Gray hath bin with 'em and threatned them if they

has ever disgraced any religious or any political party—by the story, in a few words, that the

would not come home, he would gett a party of men and fetch 'em ꝑ force. Likewise they say they have ten Indians wch went between Oxford towne and Coll. Lowe's, and that their time of return is relapsed, and are not satisfyed what is become of 'em. Whereof all these things being computed together, hath seized them with feare, butt that they were very joyfull att our comeing and were takeing up their goods to return to their habitations.

John Stanley	Wm. Dickenson
John Hawkins	Wm. Stevens
Clement Sales.	Wm. Bealey.

This is ye copy of the answer sent to the Burgesses from ye Indians.

The next discloses the nature of the charge against the Roman Catholic governors :

REPORT OF COMMITTEE OF SECRECY.

REC'D. 31 DEC. 1689.

S. P. O.
B. T. Maryland,
Vol. 1, *B. D.* 5.

The Committee of Secrecy appointed by this present Assembly, the Representative Body of this Province doe make their Report as followeth, vizt.

Wee have diligently faithfully and with all due circumspection made inquisition into the severall affaires and concernes committed to our care, for discovering of the truth thereof, and

Roman Catholics had formed a conspiracy with the Indians, to massacre the Protestants! The

we find, First, that the late Popish Governo[rs] have contrived conspired and designed by severall villanous practices and machinations, to betray their Maj[ties] Protestant subjects, of this Province, to the French, Northern, and other Indians; and that there hath been and still is eminent danger of our lives libertyes and estates, by the malitious endeavo[rs] and combinations of the said Governo[rs] with the Indians and Papists to assist in our destruction and the subversion of our Religion. And wee also find by the informations, examinations evidences and depositions by us taken, that the late Governo[rs] did prorogue and obstruct the last Assembly from meeting, least the truth of their unjust contrivances and wicked designes should be made manifest.

And wee the Committee aforesaid doe also discover and apparently find the trayterous undertakings of the said Governours in their Renunciation disowning and denying the right title and Soveraignty of King William and Queen Mary to the Crowne of England and its Dominions.

The verity of the above particulars is to be further proved by other numerous circumstances and evidences that are now in the custody of the said Committee, for their Maj[ties] service.

Read approved of and ordered to be entered in the Journall of the House of Assembly.

(*Memorandum on the back.*)

Memorandum, notwithstanding the Country have
often desired a proofe of the accusations this

testimony comes from the most respectable sources —not only from the members of the Church of

Comittee charged upon some of ye Lord Proprietaryes Deptyes, yet the same could never be obtained, or was any wayes made appear.

(*Indorsed.*)

"Report of the Comittee of Secrecy, touching the late Governmt. Copy.

"Recd fro ye Ld Baltemore, 31 Dec. 1689."

Voted in Assembly, 28 Aug., 1689.

I beg to invite especial attention to the narrative of Mrs. Smith:

NARRATIVE OF MRS. BARBARA SMITH.

30 Dec. 1689.

S. P. O.
B. T. Maryland
Vol. 1. *B. D.* 17.

The Narrative of Barbara wife of Richard Smith of Puttuxent River in Calvert County in the Province of Maryland.

Upon the 25th of March last a rumour was spread abroad about the mouth of Puttuxent River, that ten thousand Indians were come down to the Western branch of the said river. Whereupon my husband went up to the said Western branch, where he found noe Indians, but there a strong report that nine thousand were at Matapany, and at the Mouth of Puttuxent, and that they had cutt off Capt. Bournes family, and had inforted themselves at Mata-

Rome, but also from many of the most prominent Protestants of the province; including the Honor-

pany, ; which was all false. Upon these rumours the country rose in armes, but after diligent search and inquiry in all parts of the Province, this rumour was found to be only a sham, and noe Indians any where appeared to disturb or molest any the people of our Province. All which reports I doe verily beleeve were designedly spread abroad to incite the people to rise in armes as afterwards by the like sham they were induced to doe. For in the latter end of July following one Capt. Code, Coll. Jowles, Maj^r Beal, Mr. Blakiston, with some others appeared in armes, and gave for their pretence that the Papists had invited the Northern Indians to come down and cut off the Protestants, and that their descent was to be about the latter end of August when Roasting Eares were in season, & that they therefore rose in armes to secure the Magazine of Armes and Amunition and the Protestants from being cut off by the said Indians and Papists. This was their pretence to those they found very apprehensive of the said Indians; to others they said their designe was only to proclaim the King and Queen; but when the aforesaid persons with some others had gathered together a great number of People together, they then came and seized upon the Government, who withstood them first at St. Maryes in the State House where the Records are kept, whom the said Code and his party soon overcame and seized upon the Records, from thence he proceeded with his party to Matapany House wherein Coll. Darnall with some forces, as many Protestants as Papists, had garisoned themselves, but were soon forced to capitulate surrender and yield to the said Code and his party. They haveing thus possessed themselves of the governm^t, one Johnson master of a ship being bound for England, they gave him charge he should carry noe letters but what was sent from themselves, & my husband they arrested and put in

able Thomas Smyth, the ancestor of the Smyths of Trumpington, subsequently of Chestertown;

prison for fear he should goe for England with the said Johnson to give an accompt of their proceedings, and as soon as the said Johnson was gone they released him again. The said Cole and his complices then sent out letters to all the Countyes of the Province to choose an Assembly. What was done in the rest of the Countyes besides Calvert and Ann Arrundell I am not acquainted with, but when the s[d] letters for the chooseing of Burgesses came to our Sheriff to sumon the people for that purpose, he refused the same. They then went to Mr. Clegatt, Corroner, and he alsoe refused (who are both Protestants). Whereupon Coll. Jowles rode about to give the people notice himself. When the County were come together most of the Housekeepers agreed not to choose any Burgesses, and drew up an abhorrence against such proceedings; y[e] which election was alsoe much opposed by our Sheriff. Whereupon Coll. Jowles gathered his souldiers and caused the election to be made by the number he had, which was not above twenty, and of them not above ten that were capable of electing. Coll. Jowles himself and Maj[r] Beal his next officer were returned for two of the Burgesses elected, and because Mr. Tanéy, the Sheriff, & my husband endeavoured to oppose the said Election, the said Code caused them to be put in Prison. Neither for this Election nor in their cause did almost any of our county appear that were men of estates or men of note, but they to the contrary published an abhorrence against such proceedings, and were themselves, as are most of our County, Protestants. The County of Ann Arrundell, which is accounted the most populous and richest of the whole Province, and wherein is but one Papist family, unanimously stood out, and would not elect any Burgesses. About the 21st of August the Assembly of their calling met, before whom was brought Mr. Taney our Sheriff and my husband; and

from Major Joseph Wickes, at one time chief justice of the County Court, and many years a

Capt. Code and his complices haveing pretended they had the Kings Proclama[n] for what they did, my husband demanded to see the same; but their answer was, take him away, Sheriff. Mr. Taney likewise asking them by what authority he was called before them, Code answered What, this is like King Charles, and you are King Taney, take him away. Notwithstanding upon the said Code's riseing as before is said, their pretence was cheifly to secure the Country against the Indians, yet all this while nor untill my comeing away which was the 26th of September last, there was not the least appearance of any forreign or home Indians comeing to disturb us. What was their further proceedings in their Assembly I am not able to give any acco[t] of, but Mr. Taney and my husband were detained prisoner at my comeing away.

(Signed) BARBARA SMITH.

Dated in London, the 30th of December, 1689.

(Indorsed) "Mrs. Smith's Narrative of the troubles in Maryland."

The testimony from the Protestant county of Kent is exceedingly valuable:

ADDRESS OF PROTESTANTS OF KENT COUNTY.

NOVEMBER, 1689.

S. P. O.
B. T. Maryland,
Vol. 1, *B. D.* 41.

TO THE KING'S MOST EXCELLENT MAJESTIE:—

Wee your Majesties most loyall and dutyfull subjects the ancient Protestant Inhabitants of Kent County in your Maj[ties] Province of Maryland, who have here enjoyed many halcyon dayes under

distinguished representative of Kent; from the Honorable Henry De Courcy (then written *Cour-*

the imediate Governm[t] of Charles Lord Baron of Baltemore and his hon[ble] Father, absolute Lords Proprietaries of y[e] said Province by charter of your Royall Progenitors, wherein our Rights and Freedoms are so interwoven with his Lordships prerogative, that wee have allwaies had y[e] same liberties and priviledges secured to us, as other your Maj[ties] subjects in the Kingdome of England. And wee againe by vertue of the said Charter (as it enjoyned us) have alwayes paid our obedience to the said Lord Baltemore and his hon[ble] Father, by whom equally and indifferently were justice, favour, authority & preferment administered, bestowed conferred and given to and upon your Maj[ties] subjects of all perswasions: Doe in prostrate and humble manner testifie to your Ma[tie] that we abhorr & detest y[e] falsehood and unfaithfullness of John Coade and others his Associates and Agents, who first by dispersing untrue reports of prodigious armies of Indians and French Papists invadeing us, did stirr up unjust jealousies and dismall apprehensions in y[e] less cautious sort of people of this Province, and then haveing thereby created unnecessary feares & disposed y[e] people to mutiny and tumult, made further insurrection, and extorted the lawfull governm[t] from the Lord Propriet[y], who was alwayes as ready to redress our aggrievances as wee to complaine. And now the said John Coade and his accomplices haveing assumed the Government upon themselves, and procured a Convention to be tumultuously assembled, did tyrannically imprison, restrain and turn out of civill and military Comission severall of your Maj[ties] good subjects of unquestionable loyalty and affection to the Church of England, who approved nott of his actions, and who might justly by your Maj[ties] proclamation have continued in authority, and done your Maj[tie] good service. And those Delegates in that manner con-

sey), a descendant, it is strongly presumed, of an illustrious Anglo-Norman family, and a perfect

vened, (being part or most of them factious persons of no comendable life and conversation) have arbitrarily decreed and ordained many things to the inconvenience of your Majesties people, placed the Militia of severall Counties in the hands of unworthy and infamous persons; and the better to make their decrees to be observed, many of the said Delegates have procured themselves to be putt in judiciall places, to the terror of your Maj[ties] more peaceable subjects. From the dangers and apprehensions whereof, Wee your Majesties most loyall, dutyfull, and Protestant subjects, in these our Addresses humbly crave by your Princely care and prudence to be freed and enlarged, and that the Government together with your Maj[ties] favour and a lasting settlement may be again restored to the Rt. Hon[ble] Lord Baltemore, which will make him and us happy, and give us new occasion to bless God, and pray for your Maj[ties] life and happy reign.

(Signed) Wm. Frisby, Griffith Jones, Robert Burman, Philemon Hemsley, Simon Wilmer, William Peckett, Josias Lanham, Thomas Ringgold, Tho. Smyth, Henry Coursey, Josh. Wickes, Jno. Hynson, George Sturton, Lambart Wilmer, Gerrardus Wessels, Richard Jones, Philip Conner.

(*Indorsed*)

"Kent County in the Province of Maryland.
Address to His Maj[ty]."

N.B.—There are several other addresses from various Counties, with numerous signatures.

R. L.

master of the whole aboriginal diplomacy of that period; from Michael Taney, the high sheriff of

Col. Darnall was a Roman Catholic. But he surely should be allowed to speak:

COL. HENRY DARNALL'S NARRATIVE.
31 Dec., 1689.

S. P. O. B. T. Maryland, Vol. 1, *B. D.* 16.

The Narrative of Coll. Henry Darnall, late one of the Councill of the Rt. Hon[ble] y[e] Lord Proprietary of the Province of Maryland.

On the 15th of March last Coll. Jowles sent word to the Councill (then at St. Maryes) that three thousand Indians were comeing down on the Inhabitants, and were at the head of Puttuxent River, and required armes and amunition for the people to goe against the said Indians, all which was with all expedition sent him by Coll. Digges. The next morning I went up myself to Coll. Jowles, where I found them all in armes, and they told me they heard there was three thousand Indians at Matapany (from when I then came). I assured the People it was a false report, and offered myself to goe in person if they could advise me where any enemyes were, Indians or others, whereat they seemed very well satisfied. I began to suspect this was only a contrivance of some ill-minded men, who under this pretence would raise the Country, as by what happened afterwards we had reason to beleeve. Upon the most diligent search and enquiry into this whole matter, noe Indians any where appeared, and when ever any messenger was sent to the place where it was said the Indians

Calvert, and the ancestor of the present chief justice of the United States; from Richard Smith, a

were come, there the Inhabitants would tell them they heard they were landed at such a place; but after long search from place to place and noe sign of any Indians, the people were pretty well pacified, and Coll. Jowles himself wrote a Remonstrance (the copy whereof is here inclosed) which he signed, as did severall others who had the examination of this matter, the which was published in order to quiet the People, who in a few dayes seemed to be freed from their apprehensions. From this time untill the 16th of July foll. the country was all quiet and noe appearance of any enemy to disturb them, Indians or else. On the said 16th of July, a messenger came to me at Matapany, in the night time, to acquaint me that John Cood was raiseing men up Potowmeck; whereupon I informed the Councill thereof, who immediately dispatched a person to know the truth; but the said person was taken by Cood as a spy and by him kept, soe the Councill had noe notice untill two dayes of any thing, when they were assured that Cood had raised men up Potowmeck, and that some were come to him out of Charles County, who were all marching down toward St. Maryes, and in their way were joined with Maj^r Campbell and his men. Coll. Digges, haveing notice whereof, got together about an hundred men, and went into the State House at St. Maryes, which Cood and his party came to attack, and which Coll. Digges (his men not being willing to fight) was forced to surrender, wherein were the Records of the whole Province, which Cood and his party seized. In this while Maj^r Sewall and myself went up Pattuxent River to raise men to oppose said Cood and his party, where wee found most of the Officers ready to come in to us, but their men were possessed with a beleef that Cood rose only to preserve the country from the Indians & Papists, and to

brave and generous spirit, connected with the family of Somerset, and the forefather of the

proclaim the King & Queen, and would doe them noe harm, and therefore would not stir to run themselves into danger; soe that all the men we could get amounted not to one hundred and sixty, and by this time Cood's party were encreased to seaven hundred. The Councill seeing how the people were led away by false reports and shams, in order to quiet them and give them all imaginable assurance they were clear and innocent of inviteing the Indians down, as was laid to their charge, offered to make Coll. Jowles (who was the cheif of their party next to Cood) Gen[ll] of all the forces in the Province, and sent such an offer to him, who returned a very civill answere, that haveing comunicated what we wrote to his own men he had with him, they were extreamly satisfied therewith, and gave us hopes he would come down to us; but to the contrary he went & joined Cood at St. Maryes, to whom and to all then in armes there, the Councill sent a Proclamation of pardon, upon condition they would lay down their armes and repair to their respective habitations: the which Cood (as we were credibly informed) instead of reading to the People what was therein contained, read a defyance from us, thereby to enrage and not to pacify them. Cood and his party haveing thus made themselves masters of the State House & the Records at St. Maryes, borrowed some great gunns of one Captain Burnham, master of a ship belonging to London, and came to attack Matapany House, the which when he came before, he sent a Trumpeter & demanded a surrender. Wee desired a parley and personall treaty in the hearing of the People, which Cood would never consent to. We knew if we could but obtain that in the hearing of the People, we should be able to disabuse them and clear ourselves of what they were made beleeve against us; but

Smiths of St. Leonard's Creek, and of the Dulanys and the Addisons; and from Captain Thomas Claggett, the progenitor of the first Anglican bishop of Maryland. The opposition of these Protestants is, indeed, honorable, in the highest degree, to their memory. Taney was one of the

this we could never get at their hands, but to the contrary they used all possible meanes to keep the People ignorant of what we proposed or offered, and made use of such artifices as the following, to exasperate them. They caused a man to come rideing Post with a letter, wherein was contained that our neighbour Indians had cut up their corn and were gone from their towns, and that there was an Englishman found with his belly ript open, which in truth was no such thing, as they themselves owned after Matapany House was surrendred. We being in this condition and noe hopes left of quieting or repelling the People thus enraged, to prevent effusion of blood, capitulated and surrendred. After the surrender of the said house, his Lordships Councill endeavoured to send an acco[t] of these transactions by one Johnson master of a ship bound for London, to his Lordship, the which the said Johnson delivered to Cood. When we found we could send noe letters, Maj[r] Sewall and myself desired of Johnson we might have a passage in him for England, to give his Lords[p] acco[t] of matters by word of mouth, which the said Johnson refused, upon pretended orders to the contrary from Cood. Whereupon Maj[r] Sewall & myself went to Pensylvania, to endeavour to get a passage there; upon which Cood and his party to occasion to give out we were gone to bring in the Northern Indians; but we missing of a passage there, came back and stayd in Ann Arrundell County (who never had joyned with

victims of a cruel imprisonment, accompanied with gross insults and indecent taunts, in consequence of his cool and inflexible refusal to sanction the iniquitous proceedings of Col. Jowles, and the other leaders of the revolution. Smith also was a victim.

Cood and his party) until the 26th of September, when (Maj^{r} Sewall then being sick) I myself got a passage hither in one Everard. As to their proceedings in their Assembly, I can give noe acco^{t}, only that they have taken severall Prisoners.

(Signed) HENRY DARNALL.

LONDON, *December* 31*st*, 1689.

(*Indorsed*)
"Coll. Darnall's Narrative of the troubles in Maryland. 1689."

The following is from the ancestor of the Chief Justice:

MR. MICHAEL TANEY TO MRS. SMITH.

14 SEPT., 1689.

S. P. O.
B. T. Maryland,
Vol. 1, *B. D.*, 26.

MADAM SMITH :—

I doubt not but you have heard what pretence those gentlemen who have lately taken up arms here in Maryland, in their majesties' names (to pull down ye lawful authority of ye Lord Balltamore here, which he held under their said majesties), makes for my confinement in prison along with your husband, the which I

Besides Anne Arundel and Charles, six counties, between the years 1649 and 1698, were erected—

hope neither you nor any good Christian or moral honest man or woman, which ever had any acquaintance with my life and conversation, will credit; and that you and all persons to whom this shall come, may know what I have done, whereby they ground their pretence. I therefore hereafter write down y[e] heads of the whole (viz.): At the first of my knowing of their taking up arms, which was some time in July, 1689, I endeavored, with what arguments I could use, to persuade all people, but chiefly Col. Jowles (my now chief enemy), to lie still and keep the peace of y[e] country, until their majesties' pleasure should be known; for that I looked upon it to be rebellion for persons here, without order from their majesties, to take up arms against y[e] lawful authority, which then rested in y[e] lord proprietary under their majesties, as I did conceive; which arguments, with some, I presume, prevailed, so that they lay still, but not with Col. Jowles. Then afterwards, when they besieged Mattapony, I went first to the gentlemen's camp, and afterwards to Mattapony, and, as an instrument of peace, so far as I could with my weak endeavors, Mr. Marsham being with me, persuaded both parties to comply without shedding blood, and accordingly they did. At which time Mattapony by y[e] Governors being surrendered, and the magazine of arms and ammunition all over the country, as soon as they possibly they could, seized on by those gent., so that they had the strength and command of most of y[e] country in their hands; and all papists in general desisting to act any further in government and office; but Col. Jowles and y[e] rest of those gent., not content to rest there, or not thinking themselves safe in what they had done, sending out precepts in their majesties' names, requiring the sheriffs of each county to warn the people to meet together and choose delegates and representatives to meet and

four upon the eastern, and two upon the western shore. And at the period of the Protestant revo-

assemble together, under pretence of settling affairs; and also a proclamation that all officers not being papists, or having been in actual arms, nor any ways declared against their majesties' service, honor, and dignity, should continue in their places; and also a declaration of their own aggrievances to be publicly read; and Col. Jowles showing me some of those papers, being directed to me, as sheriff of Calvert County, I not being willing to execute their commands, endeavored to excuse myself, saying, I look upon myself, by y[e] surrender of y[e] government, to be discharged of my office. Whereupon Col. Jowles took some other course to have it done; but afterwards I finding most people of our county, and being informed it was so generally through y[e] country, that all people, except such as had been in arms or abetters to their cause, was willing to remain as they were, until their Majesties pleasure should be known, and I conceiving that my consenting to choose delegates and representatives to sit in such Assembly, and they countenancing the thing that was done, although they were awed to it, would make me guilty as well as they that did it; therefore I resolved not to choose, nor consent that any should be chose; however, being modest forbore railing or speaking grossly of what was done. And when the time appointed was come for y[e] election, Col. Jowles and divers of his soldiers being at y[e] place, and I also and divers of the better sort of the people of our county, discourse arose about choosing representatives, and I and many others, being much the greater number, argued against choosing any. Amongst which discourse, Col. Jowles threatened that if we would not choose representatives freely, he would fetch them down with y[e] long sword, and withall required y[e] deputy clerk to read some papers that he had. Whereupon I asked Col. Jowles whether those papers were their majesties' authority, and

lution, the population of the province, we may suppose, was not less than twenty-five thousand;

if they were I would read them myself, if not, they should not be read. But he still bid ye clerk read them. Whereupon I said to him and the rest of ye company, "Gentlemen, if the lord proprietary have any authority here, I command you, speaking to ye clerk, in ye name of ye lord proprietary, to read no papers here. Whereupon Col. Jowles went away in great rage, saying he would choose none, yet, afterwards, having got some of his soldiers to drink, he and they did somewhat which they called a free choice, and I and many more of the better sort of ye people set our hands to a paper, writing that expressed modestly and loyally some reasons why we were not willing to choose any representatives to sit in that intended assembly. For which doing I was fetched from my house on Sunday ye 25th of August, 1689, by James Bigger and six other armed men, by order of the persons assembled at ye command of Coad and his accomplices, and kept close prisoner at ye house of Philip Lynes, under a guard of armed men, and upon ye 3^d^ day of September carried by a company of soldiers before ye said Assembly, where Coad accused me of rebellion against their majesties King William and Queen Mary, for acting as above written, and withal told me if I would submit to a trial they would assign me counsel. Whereto I answered them that I was a freeborn and loyal subject to their majesties of England, and therefore expected the benefit of all those laws of England that were made for the preservation of ye lives and estates of all such persons, and therefore should not submit myself to any such unlawful authority as I take yours to be. Whereupon they demanded of me who was their majesties' lawful authority here. I answered, I was, as being an officer under ye Lord Balltamore, until their majesties' pleasure should be otherwise lawfully made known. Then they ordered the soldiers to take me away

most of the earliest settlements having been founded upon the islands of the Chesapeake, near the banks of its tributaries, or within the immediate vicinity of its shores. In 1654, the order erecting Charles upon the Patuxent, was rescinded; and Calvert established in place of it. A few years later, the county of the former name was erected upon the Potomac, and upon the Wico-

awhile, and soon after ordered my bringing in again before them, with Mr. Smith and Mr. Botler, telling us it was y[e] order of y[e] House that we must find good and sufficient security to be bound for us to answer before their majesties' commissioners and lawful authority what should be objected against us, and in the mean time be of good behavior. To which we answered, their authorities we looked upon not lawful to force us to give any bonds, and that we had estates in this country sufficient to oblige our staying to answer what any lawful authority could object against us. Then we were again ordered away to Mr. Lynes's, with a guard to keep us prisoners still, and afterwards having considered with ourselves, we informed them by Mr. Johns and several of them themselves speaking with us, that we would give them what bonds they pleased for our answering what should be objected against us by any lawful authority, leaving out the clause of good behavior, for that we knew they would make any thing they pleased breach of good behavior, and under presence of that, trouble us again at their pleasure. But that would not do, so at y[e] adjourning of y[e] Assembly we were all ordered by them to be kept in safe custody of Mr. Gillbert Clarke whom they made sheriff of Charles County, until we should give bond as above

mico; and about 1659, the extensive, now populous, rapidly-growing county of Baltimore. There is no trace of Talbot anterior to 1660. Somerset was erected in 1666; Dorchester, about 1669; and Cecil (which had mainly grown out of Herman's settlement) in the year 1674. Great doubt exists

required. Which is y[e] whole substance hitherto proceeded on, that is known to your humble servant to command.

MICH. TANEY.

September y[e] 14th, 1689.
Charlestown, in Charles
County, where we are, and
are like to remain still.

(Addressed)

To Madame Barbara
Smith. These.

Mem.—Y[e] 14th Sept[r]. 1689, Capt. Coode mustered all y[e] men of St. Mary's County at Chopticoe, and did then and there order y[t] all Protestants servants and freemen should apear there at Chopticoe y[t] day fortnight, with provision for a march into Anne Arundel County, and those y[t] were provided arms, to bring them with them, and those y[t] were not should there be furnished with y[e] country armes.

(Indorsed)

"Maryland, 1689.
Letter to Mrs. Smith
about Capt. Smith.
Rec[d] 16 Dec., 1689."

respecting the original boundaries of most of these counties. Anne Arundel, for instance, extended to Fishing Creek, some distance below its present limit; but the fact was not known to the legislature subsequently to the American Revolution; and a long, tedious, and very expensive controversy was the result. The boundary of Cecil reached to the southern extremity of Kent, in 1674. And at an earlier period, Baltimore embraced a large portion of the eastern shore, including Bohemia manor. The first courts of this county, there is strong reason to believe, were held upon the same side of the Chesapeake; and its ancient limits included the island, which received the first foot-prints of civilization upon the western shore of Maryland. Before the year 1689, many tracts were taken up in Prince George's; but that extensive county, out of which Frederick was carved as late as 1748, was not itself erected out of portions of Calvert and Charles till the year 1695. The names of our early counties are not unworthy of a notice. They suggest or commemorate interesting facts, in the history of our colonization.

Spesutia Island, originally within the limits of Baltimore, perpetuates the name of Col. Nathaniel Utye, one of the most sanguine and adventurous pioneers in the colonization of the country, upon the head-waters of the Chesapeake. There, also, did Augustine Herman make his treaty with the Indian chiefs, for his title to the land upon the Bohemia River. Spesutia has sometimes been confounded with the island, upon which Clayborne established his trading-post with the Susquehannocks, as early as 1630. But Watson's is the one which corresponds with Palmer's in size, and in every other particular.

In duration as well as the difficulty of arriving at a satisfactory result, the contest between Anne Arundel and Calvert was not unlike that between Lord Baltimore and the Penns. But the identity of Marsh's (the admitted boundary) with Fishing Creek, is clearly proved by the records in the Land Office. And the history of the title to "Major's Choice" taken up by the Honorable Thomas Marsh, near the cliffs of Calvert, will readily develop all the evidence upon this knotty question.

CHAPTER IX.

The State of Society, from 1634 to 1689.

THE overthrow of the proprietary's authority was the knell to the hopes of St. Mary's; and, before the lapse of many more years, Annapolis became the seat of government.

During the era of Roman Catholic toleration, the original tenant of the forest lived almost side by side, and generally upon terms of the best amity, with our early colonial forefathers. Half-breeds, or their near descendants, probably still exist, both in the neighborhood of the Piscataway, and upon one or more rivers of the Eastern Shore. It has also been a thousand times asserted, that the blood of aboriginal chiefs is now represented by the Brents, by the Goldsboroughs, and by many of our other most distinguished families.

Of the *Chesapeakes* (the nation who had given a name to our "Great Bay") no vestige in Maryland appeared, at the arrival of Governor Calvert. Long before the settlement at St. Mary's, they were a small tribe, with not more than a hundred warriors, living upon a branch of the Elizabeth river, and under the dominion of the *Powhatans*, a powerful confederacy embracing more than thirty different nations, and which had extended its sway to the very banks of the Patuxent.[1]

The *Yoacomicos* lived upon the St. Mary's. They were there at the arrival of the Pilgrims. The scene between Governor Calvert and the chiefs of this tribe, has been described, not only by eye-witnesses, but also by a host of later writers. It is not more honorable to the religion of the Roman Catholic, than to the instinct of the savage. A cup of cold water, we are taught, is not without its reward; and the welcome given by these simple children of the wilderness, deserves to be held by the succeeding generations of Maryland, in the most grateful and enduring remembrance.[2]

[1] See Smith's History of Virginia; Bozman's History of Maryland.

[2] See ante, pp. 46–47. For further particulars see "A Relation of Maryland," and also Father White's Journal.

At an early period, the *Matapeaks* lived upon Kent Island. Their name is still perpetuated by a small stream. And upon the farm held by the late General Emory, is "The Indian Spring." There also was a large number of arrow-heads, and other relics. And in the same part of the island, is a neck of land, which for a long time, bore the name of *Matapax*.[1]

The *Susquehannocks*, who gave their name to a large tributary of the Chesapeake, were the most powerful confederacy within the limits of Maryland. Their chief dwelling-place was upon the head waters of the Chesapeake; but they overran a large portion of the Eastern and of the Western shore; and even invaded the *Yoacomicos*. They were also distinguished for their noble, gigantic size; and received with great kindness, Capt. Smith and his companions, during his exploration of the Chesapeake, long before the settlement upon Kent Island. Many also were the treaties, which they

[1] For several facts relating to the Indians upon this Island, see my paper presented about three years since to the Md. Historical Society.

signed with Maryland; including the one[1] for a large portion of our territory.[2]

[1] This was signed (see Bozman, vol. 2. p. 683), in 1652, at the river Severn, by Richard Bennett, Edward Lloyd, William Fuller, Thomas Marsh, and Leonard Strong, the commissioners on the part of Maryland; and by *Sawahegeh*, *Auroghtaregh*, *Scarhuhadigh*, *Ruthchogah*, and *Natheldianeh*, the chiefs on behalf of the *Susquehannocks*. The treaty ceded to Maryland all the land from the Patuxent to Palmer's Island, and from the Choptank to the Elk; but did not embrace Kent Island, nor Palmer's (now Watson's) Island. See also their treaty with Augustine Herman, Appendix, No. 2.

[2] The *Patuxents*, whose principal seat was upon the river which perpetuates their name, included a large number of little nations and tribes, remarkable for the friendliness of their feelings. The territory of the *Piscataways*, whose prominent chief bore the title of *Emperor*, was bounded, in one direction, by the country of the *Susquehannoks*; in another, by the region of the *Patuxents*. It also embraced a part of the country bordering upon the Patapsco, and upon the Potomac; including Piscataway creek, and probably the sites both of Washington and of Baltimore. Upon the Sassafras lived the *Tockwhoghs*, quite a considerable tribe, and more ferocious than many of the other Indians. Near the mouth of the Chester was a very small one, which bore the name of *Ozenics*. Both these tribes disappeared at a very early period. The former was probably absorbed by the *Susquehannoks*.

Further towards the South, on the same shore of the Chesapeake, dwelt also, at a very early period, the *Kuskarawoaks*, the great makers of *peake* and *roanoke* (the money of the Indians), and the chief "*merchants*" of aboriginal Maryland—subsequently represented by two considerable confederacies, under the names of *Choptank* and *Nanticoke*, which are still borne by the large and

The *Accomacs*, and some other tribes further South than the *Kuskarawoaks*, fell within the wide domain of the *Powhatans*.

But North of the Province, was the still more warlike and powerful confederacy, consisting of the

beautiful rivers, upon which they lived. The *peake* was more valuable than the *roanoke*. But they both consisted of shell—the former of the *conch*, the latter of the *cockle*—wrought into the shape of beads.

With the Indians upon the Delaware, also, we entered into treaties. To this race belonged, it is supposed, the *Ozenies*, with some other tribes of Maryland. And a chief was held, for his virtues, in such profound veneration, not only by the Red man, but also by the White; and his memory is so closely interwoven with the traditions and recollections of our ancestry; that I cannot close this sketch, without the mention of his name. To the Aborigines upon the Delaware, he appeared, indeed, in the same light as did Alfred to the English, or St. Louis to the French. Rising above the level of his own kindred, he became also the representative of a sympathy (how hard was it to realize a union!) between the disciples of civilization and the children of barbarism. And, in token of the companionship, societies were formed, both in Maryland and elsewhere, some time before the American Revolution; and, in May, celebrated their anniversaries, with the Indian war-dance, and other ceremonies. At a little later period, a larger one was organized, representing the thirteen original States of the North American confederacy. And the Hall of *St. Tammany*, in the City of New York, now devoted to the purposes of a mere political party, is still, in its highest and most historical sense, a monument to the memory of the illustrious chief of the *Delawares*.

Mohawks, and of four other nations;[1] whose chief dwelling place was upon the rivers of New York; but who not unfrequently descended the Susquehannah, and spread the greatest alarm among the colonists.[2] The relations, both at peace and at war, with this formidable confederacy, constitute (if we except the labors of the missionaries) the most interesting and important portion of the Aboriginal History of Maryland. The highest diplomatic skill was also exerted. And to the services of the Honorable Philemon Lloyd, but especially of the Honorable Henry De Courcy, both at Albany and elsewhere, was the proprietary, so many years, indebted, not only for the peace of his province, but also for the lives of many of his subjects. The treaties of these faithful and estimable commissioners with the chiefs of the Five Nations (who were called *Iroquois* by the French), elicited the strongest and most significant testimonials both from the Governor and from the Assembly of Maryland. And, in the Documen-

[1] Called sometimes "The Northern Indians." See ante, *e. g.*, p. 89.

[2] Witness, also, the ill-founded panic of 1689, ante, pp. 87–105.

tary Histories of New York, some of them have been lately printed, at the expense, and through the noble energy (I blush to add) of the New Yorkers.[1] They are written in the rich, metaphorical style of the Indian.

[1] The De Courcys of My-Lord's-Gift (including Mrs. Mitchell of the Western shore), and the De Courcys of Cheston (see ante, p. 83), are representatives of the family of the Hon. Henry De Courcy. Mrs. May, the wife of the Hon. Henry May, is also a descendant of this family.

The claim of the De Courcys of Cheston (ante, p. 95) to the titles and estates of the old Anglo-Norman barony of Courcy and Kingsale, has never been tested by a judicial or by a parliamentary investigation. But the daughters of Gerald (the baron, who died about the middle of the last century) expressed the opinion, that a member of the family at Cheston was clearly entitled; and said, their impression had been derived (they spoke upon the point very positively) from their own father, before the period of his alleged insanity, or the date of the will, in which he selected Myles, of Rhode Island, as the successor. These, and many other interesting facts, upon the subject, may be found in The De Courcy Papers now held by Doct. William Henry De Courcy, of Cheston, the brother of the Hon. Mrs. May. Of the high social rank of this family, at the very period of their arrival, the letter of Mr. Secretary Hatton is sufficient evidence. See note to the sketch of Mr. Hatton's life.

It is generally supposed, the Hon. Henry De Courcy was a Roman Catholic. The inference has been drawn, I presume, from the fact of his extreme intimacy with Lord Baltimore, and from his uniform support of the principles, upon which the proprietary's

Under that mild form of the feudal polity, which from the first prevailed in Maryland, our ancestors held their lands as a gift from the proprietary, bore a willing allegiance, and paid a very small rent. Their title, indeed, for all practical purposes, was equivalent to a fee-simple. A little tract was given to each emigrant; and an additional quantity for every person he had brought, or subsequently transported. Tracts of a thousand acres and upwards were erected into manors, under the proprietary, with the right given to the lords of these limited territories, to hold courts-baron and courts-leet. And we have the recorded evidence of the fact, that upon St. Gabriel's, and St. Clement's, it was exercised. The lord proprietary also, who held the whole province, by fealty, of the English crown, pledged himself to deliver, every year, "on Tuesday, in Easter week," at the royal castle of Windsor, "two Indian arrows," and a fifth of "all the gold and silver," which might be "found."

government was conducted. It can easily be proved, however, that he was a Protestant. Nor was he the only Protestant cavalier, whose magnanimity and high sense of justice had induced him, with so much zeal, to sustain the proprietary's cause.

The government, in every essential particular, was a monarchy. Of this, the charter is sufficient evidence. It is true, the proprietary was a subject of the English crown. But, under the feudal state of society, it was not unusual for one prince to hold his territory of another. Scotland was once a fief of England; and King John a vassal of the Pope of Rome. But no powers were ever exercised with a more substantial regard for the welfare of the colonists. And practical liberty did exist, at the very foundation of the colony.

The privy councillors, and the lords of manors formed the class,[1] in which we find the germ of a nobility. Below them, was a considerable number of planters, who bore the title of gentlemen—as large a class[2] in Maryland, as in any other Anglo-American colony—and the greater part of them,

[1] The high Provincial Court was analogous to that of the King's Bench; and constituted the original of our present Court of Appeals. For many years, the governor or lord proprietary, and the privy councillors, sat upon its bench.

[2] From them, also, were taken the early county court judges, originally styled justices and commissioners. They had, also, much of the jurisdiction subsequently given to the levy courts, and to the orphans' courts; and personally were held in the very highest esteem.

during the first twenty years, probably Roman Catholics. Upon the small manors (those held by the colonists) were the tenants, usually styled freeholders and suitors; and who, unlike the gentlemen, rarely had the prefix of *Mr.*

Three kinds of servitude prevailed—but, all of them, mild in their character; and honorable, in a high degree, to the master. Many emigrants, who had come under an indenture, performed a faithful service; and then received their discharge, with a comfortable outfit. A few Indians, also, were held in a state of slavery. And negro slaves, although not many of them, were introduced, during the earliest period of our history. Subsequently to the Protestant Revolution, convicts from England, it is certain, were imported.

No towns of any commercial importance arose, during the first sixty years. St. Mary's was never large. And the only edifice of any pretension was the State House. The foundation of Annapolis was laid. That city (then called a landing), and the one projected upon South River, were erected into ports of entry, in 1683. And, on the Eastern shore, were the little towns of New-Yarmouth and York; the former upon a branch of the Chester; the latter, it is supposed, upon some part of the Wye.[1] But the necessity for many towns did not then exist. The most striking feature upon the face of society was the plantations. Upon them, were held some of our earliest courts and councils. Hardly a home, or a tenement was not approached by water. And our governors, privy councillors, and county court judges were, all of them, planters. The principal planters were also the merchants, who traded with London, and the other great ports of England. And the large plantations, with their group of store-houses and other buildings, assumed the appearance, and performed the office of little towns.

The currency of the province presents a good key to the state of society. In some contracts, none was required. There was simply a barter, or an exchange of one commodity for another. In commercial transactions, a little English or European coin was occasionally used. In the trade with the Indians, for beaver-skins and other valuable

[1] Charleston, the original county seat of Prince George's, but founded long before the erection of that county, stood at the fork of the Patuxent, either near or upon the site of Mount Calvert.

articles, the *peake* and the *roanoke* obtained a free circulation; and a good deal of this kind of currency was held by the colonists. There was also a provincial coin, consisting of silver, and issued by the proprietary, of various denominations (as groats, sixpences, and shillings), having upon one side his lordship's arms, with the motto *Crescite et Multiplicamini*, upon the other his image, with the circumscription *Cæcilius Dominus Terræ-Mariæ, &c.*; being equal, in fineness, to English sterling, and of the same standard, though somewhat less in weight. Specimens of this curious money are preserved;[1] very little of which, there is reason to believe, was ever coined—tobacco being the most common currency of the province; and one pound of it, in 1650, worth about three-pence of English money.

Our ancestors generally sat upon stools[2] and

[1] I have seen one or two in the possession of the Maryland Historical Society, presented, I am informed, by our generous countryman, Mr. Peabody, of London.

[2] I have seen several chairs. But stools and forms were chiefly used. The form was a sort of bench; and sometimes, if not always, attached to the wall. The few chairs were, most of them, made of iron, and covered with leather. They were considered the best.

forms; dined without forks;[1] but made a free use of the napkin; and paid especial attention to the furniture of their bed-chambers. The walls also of their principal rooms were wainscoted.[2] And they kept a great deal of rich and massive silver plate, upon which were carved the arms of their own ancestry. Tea and coffee they rarely, if ever, tasted. Sugar they sometimes had. But freely did they drink both cider, and sack. And there is frequent mention of the silver sack-cup. Strong punch and sack, it would seem, were their favorite drinks.[3]

[1] Their tables were oval. I was upon the eve of adding, our forefathers usually cut their meat with their rapiers, or other weapons; for I have rarely met with dinner-knives. And I have examined a hundred inventories, without finding a single fork. I doubt, if there was one, in the whole province, the first thirty years. Nor should the fact surprise us. If we look at Beckmann's History of Inventions (I am obliged to an old schoolmate, for so good an authority), we will see, that this article was introduced into society at a late period.

[2] Specimens of the wainscoted wall are still preserved at some of the old family seats in Maryland. They have been much admired; and, in England, are again becoming fashionable.

[3] Sack was the special favorite. A case, *e. g.*, is referred for an arbitration to the Hon. Thomas Marsh, who, in giving his award, added "a hogshead of sack" *to be drunk* between the parties. Take another :—Gov. Calvert ordered Col. Price to bring various articles to Fort St. Inigo's, for the use of the soldiers. "And

They had also every variety of fruit, both for the winter, as well as for the summer. They delighted in pears and apricots, in figs and pomegranates,[1] in peaches and apples, and the most luscious melons. The wild strawberry and the grape-vine grew also, in the richest profusion. Many of the hills were covered with vines; and we have the proof, that vineyards also were cultivated. The air and the forest abounded in game; the rivers and bays in fish. Our ancestors feasted upon the best oysters of America; and dined, we may suppose, upon the Canvass-back, the most delicious duck in the world.

Providence was "not content with food to nourish man." All nature then was "music to the ear," or "beauty to the eye." The feathered songsters of the forest were constantly heard. And so fascinated were our forefathers with a bird they had never seen before their arrival, that they gave it the name of *Baltimore*—its colors (black and yel-

upon motion of sack," says the witness (see Thos. Hebden's Deposition, Lib. No. 2, p. 354), "the said governor replied, bidding him to bring sack if he found any." It occurs more frequently upon the records of the province, than upon the pages of Shakspeare.

[1] See Ogilby's America—a very interesting work—from which many of the facts in this chapter are taken.

low) corresponding with those upon the escutcheon of the Calverts. The eagle also, which still lingers, was then more frequently seen, in all his proudest majesty.

Tobacco was the great product of the province. In all the parts of Maryland at that time colonized, was it cultivated. And it is said, upon good authority, that "a hundred sail of ships," a year, from the West Indies and from England, traded in this article—the source also of a very large revenue to the English crown, at "his lordship's vast expense, industry, and hazard." Indian corn (or "mayz"), was also cultivated at an early period. From the Indians also did we obtain the sweet *potato.* The word, itself, is derived from them. So also are *pone*, *hominy*, *pocoson*, and many others.

No regular post was established; and it is doubtful, if we had any printing-press before the year 1689. Gentlemen travelled on horseback by land; or in canoes, or other small boats by water. Ferries over the rivers and other large streams, were erected by the government; and kept by the most respectable colonists—the duties, in most cases, however, being performed by their deputies. Letters were sent by private hand; and despatches from the government by a special messenger.

The practice of partaking of ardent spirits, and other refreshments, at funerals, was brought by our earliest ancestors from their own father-land; and generally, if not universally observed. The sums expended in "hot waters," and other drinks, upon such sad occasions, were surprisingly large.

The costume, during the reign of Charles the First, bore the marks of the strong military spirit of that age; and was the most striking and picturesque ever worn in England. We have also, here and there, a glimpse of it, upon the records of this province. The inventory of Thomas Egerton, a cavalier, may illustrate a part of it. There we have the falchion, and the rapier; the cloth coat lined with plush, and the embroidered belt; the gold hat-band, and the feather; the pair of shoes, and the silk stockings; the pair, also, of cuffs, and the silk garters. The signet-ring is also mentioned, one of the articles of a gentleman, at that period. And we find, that leather breeches, and stockings of the same material, were frequently worn.[1] The large

[1] Boot hose-tops, it appears, were also worn, about 1650. For Mr. Egerton's Inventory, see the Records of the Land-Office; and

collar was succeeded by the cravat, it would seem, about the time of the Protestant Revolution. Buff coats were also worn as early as 1650. The cocked hat was probably not introduced before the year 1700.

Finger-rings were worn by almost all the early landed gentry of Maryland. And they were the favorite tokens of regard and remembrance, given in their wills. The number bequeathed, during the first hundred years after the settlement at St. Mary's, would seem incredible to any one, who is not familiar with our early testamentary records. The preceding facts, in relation to dress, and including finger-rings, are predicated mainly of the Anglican and the Roman Catholic colonists.

Cattle-stealing never prevailed in Maryland to the same extent as it did in Scotland. But a governor of Virginia was convicted; and we had many cases in this province. A high sheriff of Kent was tried; and, notwithstanding his acquittal, the evidence was very strong. The witnesses stated, that the bullock was eaten in "hugger-mugger;" that a sentinel kept watch; and that Capt. Thomas Bradnox, the gentleman accused, had ordered one

for some of the articles of a lady's dress, see note, in this volume, upon the will of Mrs. Fenwick, p. 215.

of them to say nothing of the subject to the Governor of Maryland, whose visit was soon afterwards expected. Capt. Bradnox[1] was the friend, also, of Mr. Secretary Hatton.

No execution for witchcraft, under the sentence of a court, has ever marred, it would seem, the annals of this province. But Mary Lee, during a stormy passage upon the high seas, was put to death by a company of sailors. And we have at least one case of conviction. It is that of John Cowman, given in Ridgely's Annals of Annapolis.

Mr. Macaulay says, that many English gentlemen and lords of manors, as late as 1685, had hardly "learning enough to sign" a *mittimus*. The accuracy of his picture has been doubted. But so far as it regards the education of many of the early gentry of Maryland, nothing could be more faithfully drawn.[2] We have instances here, in which the servant writes his name, and the master makes his mark. Capt. Bradnox was wholly ignorant of the art of writing. And one, if not

[1] For the law relating to cattle-marks, see this volume, p. 226.

[2] That many gentlemen could not write their names, is evident. They repeatedly make their marks. Cases from the Record could be cited.

several of the earliest judges of the provincial court, came within the same category. The fact, indeed, suggests a very important inference; and can only be accounted for upon the true historical hypothesis. In the past, we see the military; in the present, the commercial spirit of society. Knights, and not merchants, were once the gentlemen of England. The sword, and not the purse or the pen, was still the emblem of power. And it would be a great mistake to suppose, the unlettered gentlemen of two hundred years ago, were not persons either of intelligence, or of lofty bearing. The ancestors of these men had been upon many a bloody battle-field; and a living tradition had supplied the place of history. No class was more jealous of the honor of their families; or the glory of their country. The landed gentlemen of England, from whom many of our own early gentry derived their origin, were, themselves, the descendants, through younger branches, of the old and powerful aristocracy of that kingdom; and felt the highest pride in all that is grand, chivalrous, or glorious, in the annals of that great country; for the period of a thousand years.

Between the morals of the past, and those of the

present, it would be impossible to draw a full or fair contrast. But injustice, in this particular, has certainly been done to the memory of our ancestors; and the letter of Parson Yeo to the Archbishop, in 1676, is little better than a libel. Without wishing to throw a veil over the sins of the past, or excuse in the least its rudeness or its violence; I have no hesitation in expressing the opinion, for whatever it may be worth, that in the sincerity of their friendships, in the depth of their religious convictions, in the strength of their domestic affections, and in a general reverence for things sacred, our forefathers far outshine the men of this generation, with all its pomp and pride of civilization.

Nor must we forget the new element which was introduced into the early society of Maryland—the element of religious liberty—an element, which we cannot but suppose, constantly exerted its influence in enlarging the mind, and elevating the thought of the colonists—an active principle in the life of the early planters—the crowning glory of the era, in which they lived. Nor did it die, at the fall of St. Mary's, or the overthrow of the proprietary. It had taken root in other parts of the continent. And its fruit we now enjoy.

CHAPTER X.

The Law-givers of 1649—Their Names—A fragment of the Legislative Journal.

THE claim of the Roman Catholic legislators has been either denied or doubted by so many respectable writers;[1] and so much obscurity has

[1] I will name but four:—the Honorable John Pendleton Kennedy, whose various contributions to our literature have conferred a lasting obligation upon the friends of historical learning; the late John Leeds Bozman, whose history (a book of high authority) was published by the State; Mr. Sebastian F. Streeter, in his "Two Hundred Years Ago," distinguished not less for its general accuracy of statement than for the noble zeal of its author in the prosecution of some of the most difficult inquiries within the whole range of our early history; and the Rev. Ethan Allen, whose "Maryland Toleration" is favorably received by the public, especially by the clergy and laity of the Protestant Episcopal church. More than a century after the passage of the important act, Mr. Chalmers wrote the celebrated "Annals," in which he states the Assembly was "composed chiefly of Roman Catholics." But he did not give the proof; nor does Mr. Bancroft, or any other historian. Mr. McMahon, the highest authority upon the history of Maryland, abstains (I think rather

really hung (for the journal is lost) over the faith, and identity (including the very names) of the members; that no apology, it is hoped, will be demanded by the truth-loving reader, for the tediousness of the following details.

Fortunately for the settlement of the question, a fragment of the legislative journal is still preserved (strangely enough!) upon the records of the Land Office. It consists of a report from the financial committee; and the action of the Assem-

studiously) from the expression of any very clear opinion. But while I do not feel it safe, upon some questions, to follow Mr. McSherry, the Roman Catholic, it is but due to him to say, in simplicity and beauty of style, in freshness of thought, and the general fascination with which he invests his subject, he has excelled all the historians of this State; and that in reading his book, I was, for the first time in my life, inspired with a taste for the study of our early provincial annals. The Georgetown College *MS.* for a copy of which I am indebted, through the kindness of Governor Lowe, to President Stonestreet, is a much older production, judging from its internal evidence, than any of the published writings of Mr. Chalmers; but not only without a date or the name of its author, but also unsatisfactory in many other respects. With perfect candor, I will now add, that the best argument I have seen in favor of the Roman Catholic claim, is from the pen of my good and dear friend, Wm. Meade Addison. It yet remains for me, by God's help, to try my own hand.

bly in relation to "The Bill of Charges."[1] If we add to it a part of the journal of the following

[1] The Report which follows contains the name of every Burgess:

"Saturday, the 21st of April, 1649, being ye last day and sessions-day of the Assembly—the House being called, all assembled but Mr. Pile and Mr. Hatton, whose absence was excused by the governor. The committee brought in the charge of this present Assembly, which is as followeth, viz.—At the committee for charges of the Assembly, the committee appointed the sums under-written to be paid to the parties under-written this 21st of April, 1649—all tobacco under-written due with cask.

	Tob.
Imprimis, for the shallop and one man 9 days, . . .	200
For one man 8 days, ...	080
For two men, seven days, ...	140
For provisions for the men paid by the sheriff,. . .	100
For fetching wood and water during this Assembly, . .	150
	670
Hereof Kent is to pay a sixth part being . . .	112
St. Mary's county is to pay the rest, being, . .	558
	000
Lieut. Banks, Walter Peake, Mr. Browne, and John Maunsell, for their diet, at 16lb. Tob. per day a man for twenty-one days and for loss of their time, 10lb. Tobacco per day, with cask,	000 2184 000
Mr. Thornborough, for 21 days, ...	210
George Manners, for 16 days, ...	160
To Mr. Fenwick for his trouble at this Assembly, ...	1200
For Mr. Bretton, ...	210
For Capt. Vaughan for going to the eastern shore, and sending down a boat and hands to St. Mary's, ...	500
For the clerk of the Assembly, for 25 days, at 50lb. per day. .	1250

year,[1] and the facts already given by Bozman and other historians, it will be easy for us to ascertain,

The sixth part of which 1250 Kent is to pay . . .	208
St. Mary's county to pay the rest, being	1042
For Mr. Conner for the charge of this Assembly, . . .	1342

The committee finding it just to be levied per poll, as we conceive.

Cuthbert Fenwick,	Philip Conner,
Richard Banks.	Richard Browne,
	Walter Peake.

See Land Records, Lib. No. 2, pp. 488–489.

[1] "April 29th, 1650.—We, whose names are hereunder written, declare, that our intents in passing the *Bill* the last year, entitled an Act for the support of the Lord Proprietary (and do verily believe, that the intention of the whole House then was), that these words in the law, viz., '*touching the late recovery and defence of the province*,' is only meant thereby, that those soldiers who came up in person with Governor Calvert, deceased, out of Virginia, and those others who were hired into the Fort of St. Migo's, for the defence and preservation of the province, and government reassumed by him; and other just arrears incurred during that time in the said Fort, should be satisfied by virtue of that Act; and no others. Wm. Stone, Thos. Green, John Price, John Pile, Thomas Hatton, Robert Vaughan, Cuthbert Fenwick, William Bretton, George Manners, Robert Clarke.

"29th April *predict.* It is thought fit by both Houses of this present Assembly, that the act above-mentioned be understood and judged upon according to the intentions expressed in the declaration above-written. Concurred, *ut supra.* Assented *ut supra.*

Land Records, Lib. No. 3, p. 345.

beyond the shadow of a doubt, who were the Assemblymen of 1649.[1]

[1] The inference from the preceding fragment of 1649 is fully established by the analogy drawn from the Journal of 1650—remembering, however, that Mr. Fenwick took the place of Doctor Mathews (see Bozman), and (what is also well known) that Messrs. Cox and Puddington were sent from Anne Arundel county.

"Return from the Sheriff of St. Mary's, 2d of April, 1650.

"All and every the freemen of St. Mary's county have been summoned, according to the direction of those summons, and have made choice of these burgesses following for every hundred, viz.:—

For St. George's hundred,	Mr. John Hatch, Mr. Walter Beane.
For Newtown hundred,	Mr. John Medley, Mr. Wm. Brough, Mr. Robert Robins.
For St. Clement's hundred,	Mr. Francis Posey.
For St. Mary's hundred,	Mr. Philip Land, Mr. Francis Brooks.
For St. Inigo's hundred,	Mr. Thomas Matthews.
For St. Michael's hundred,	Mr. Thomas Sterman, Mr. George Manners.

"Which I humbly certify, in return hereof.

NICHOLAS GWYTHER."

See Land Records, Lib. No. 3, p. 47.

"*Return from Kent, April*, 5, 1650.

"These summons were duly executed, and by virtue thereof, I was by the major part of the freemen, chosen burgess for the Isle of Kent county, which I do certify, in return hereof.

"ROBERT VAUGHAN."

Land Records, Lib. No. 3, p. 47.

It will be remembered, that Cecilius, the proprietary, notwithstanding his residence in England,

Common Charges to be levied by equal Assessment through ye whole Province. April 27th.

"The committee brought in the country's charge,

For Wm. Lewis, for his attendance and bringing down Indians last year,	0400
For Matthias Briant for carrying ye governor's letter,	0100
For pressing Mr. Chappel's boat,	0200
For Francis Martinson, for going to Anne Arundel and Kent counties,	0600
For the clerk of the Assembly, for 24 days at 50lb. per day,	1200
For Philip's attendance on the burgesses, &c.,	0420
For ye Sheriff, for his attendance on the House,	0500
	3420

Same Lib., p. 59.

"*The Committee's Bill of Charges, this Assembly, brought in 27th April. Allowing:—*

St. Mary's,

To	Robert Robins, for 27 days' attendance, at 50lb. per day,	1350
	Mr. Wm. Brough, for 21 days, at 50lb. per day,	1050
	John Medley, for 14 days, " "	0700
To	Mr. Philip Land, 26 days, " "	1300
To	John Hatch, 24 days, " "	1200
	Walter Beane, 24 days, " "	1200
To	Francis *Poesey*, 28 days, at 50lb. per day,	1400
To	George Manners, 21 days,	1050
	Mr. Thomas Sterman, 21 days,	1050
To	Mr. Cuthbert Fenwick, 11 days,	0550

"As for that Mr. Francis Brooks was not able, through sickness, to attend the House, and drawing of his wine, the committee think fit not to provide for him at all.

Kent,

To Capt. Robert Vaughan, for 40 days, at 50lb. per day,	2000
To boat and hand, &c.,	0250

possessed an important part of the law-making power. It is certain, the "Act" relating to "Religion" received his approval. Under the provisions of the charter, it could not have become a law, in the proper sense, without his sanction, either expressed or implied. We know he approved it. And the fact is undisputed.

Capt. Wm. Stone, it is also known, was the proprietary's lieutenant-general, or governor of the province. And the governor, at that period, was *ex-officio* the president of the privy council. His concurrence also in the passage of the Act, is a matter of record.

And we have the well-known commission of four privy councillors:—Thos. Green, John Price, John

Anne Arundel,

To Mr. Puddington, " Mr. Coxe,	for 37 days apiece, at 50lb. per day, .	3700
Boat, hands, and wages, ...		0600

"This assessment to be laid on the hundreds and counties, proportionably, every county and hundred bearing their particular charge of their own particular burgess or burgesses.

"The committee finding already 3420 lb. more of tobacco upon common charge, besides what will hereafter be reckoned. Whereupon (not be able to make a true estimate of the people inhabiting in the several counties, whereby to proportionate the

Pile, and Robert Vaughan. Robert Clark was, at the same time, the surveyor-general; and Thomas Hatton, the secretary of the province. It was the practice of these high officers, to sit in the Assembly with the councillors. And we have the proof, that they did so, in 1649.[1]

Nine burgesses represented Kent and St. Mary's. Their names are:—Cuthbert Fenwick, Philip Conner, William Bretton, Richard Browne, George Manners, Richard Banks, John Maunsell, Thomas Thornborough, and Walter Peake.

Including the governor, there were sixteen members, in the whole Assembly. Of the six privy councillors, Robert Vaughan was the only one who resided in Kent. And Philip Conner represented the freemen of that county.

assessment equally) they refer the making thereof unto the meeting in October for that purpose.

Signed,

John Price,	James Cox,
Robert Vaughan,	Philip Land,
John Hatch,	Robert Robins,
Wm. Brough	George Puddington."

Same Lib., pp. 60, 61.

[1] They signed the certificate prefixed to the Declaratory Act of 1650.

CHAPTER XI.

Their Faith—They sit in One House.

THE proprietary was a Roman Catholic; and the governor, a Protestant. Three of the privy councillors (Thomas Green, John Pile, and Robert Clarke), held the faith of the former; the other three (John Price, Robert Vaughan, and Thomas Hatton), with equal certainty, may be classed with the latter law-giver.

As the result of the strictest historical criticism—of the most careful and exhausting analysis of the whole evidence—it is but right to say, the proof is not discoverable, that more than two members of the whole House of burgesses (or representatives of the people) were either Protestants, or in direct sympathy with the Protestant class of colonists. That Mr. Conner and Capt. Banks belonged to that class, is a matter of evidence. And there is some degree of probability that Mr. Browne also held the faith of the English church. But it is certain, that five of the burgesses (Messrs. Fenwick, Bretton, Manners, Maunsell, and Peake) cherished a faith in the Roman church; and we have the basis of a very strong presumption, that Mr. Thornborough (a sixth member of this House) was also a Roman Catholic.

Including the proprietary and Mr. Thornborough, ten of the law-givers of 1649 held the faith of the Roman Catholic Church. If we count the governor and the two burgesses; six, it will appear, belonged to some branch of the Protestant—probably the Anglo-Catholic. Adding Mr. Browne, we have a seventh. But this is a superficial view of the question; and refers only to the time, they all sat in one House.

CHAPTER XII.

The Whole Strength of the Roman Catholic Element in the Assembly.

All, we have from the remaining parts of the journal, is that on the "last day" of the Assembly, the representatives of the freemen, with the governor, and with the privy councillors (excepting Messrs. Pile and Hatton), assembled in one "House;" and that, on the same day, was passed the "Act concerning Religion."[1] It can be proved from the records, that of the fourteen, eight (including Mr. Thornborough) were Roman Catholics; and six (with Mr. Browne) were Protestants. But this estimate does not render strict historical justice to the claim of the former. The privy councillors were, all of them, as well as the governor, the special representatives of the Roman Catholic

[1] In the marginal note to the copy of the Act upon the Records of the Land Office, the date of its passage is given.

proprietary;[1] under an express pledge imposed by him, shortly before the meeting of the Assembly (as may be seen from the official oath), to do nothing at variance with the religious freedom of any believer in Christianity; and removable, any moment, at his bidding. It would be fairer, therefore, to place the governor and the four privy councillors on the same side as the six Roman Catholic burgesses. Giving Mr. Browne to the other side, we have eleven Roman Catholic against three Protestant votes.

[1] This fact is presented, in a very forcible light, by Mr. Addison. See Addison's Religious Toleration in America.

CHAPTER XIII.

The Burgesses, as a Distinct Branch of the Legislature—A Majority of Roman Catholic Representatives.

But there is the strongest evidence to show, that at a previous stage of the session, the Assembly sat in two Houses. This is the opinion of Bozman, who is, by no means, partial towards the Roman Catholics—an opinion sustained also by Chalmers, by Bacon, and by Bancroft. It is evident that Mr. Fenwick received an extra allowance.[1] May we not suppose, he was the chief officer, or speaker, of the Lower House? But the best argument is drawn from the analogy furnished by the Assembly of the following year; and by the very phraseology, in the Act relating to religion. We know the Legislature of 1650, although expressly divided into two distinct chambers, sat near the end of the session, in one House.[2] And, in the

[1] See the Bill of Charges, ante, p. 130.

[2] The journal of 1650 has been preserved. It is in Lib. No. 3,

Act, of which we are speaking, there is a clear reference to an Upper and Lower House.[1] If we suppose, therefore (what cannot admit of a reasonable doubt), that the Act passed each House before its final adoption by the whole Assembly in one body; and still give Mr. Browne to the Protestants; we will find there were six Roman Catholics (including Mr. Thornborough) against three only of the other class of delegates.

in the Land Office. And there is abundant evidence to show that many of the laws and orders of that year were passed by "both Houses" sitting in one. I have now before me an extract from p. 61, which distinctly states, that on the "29th" of April, the "burgesses of the Lower House being sent for, came and joined themselves with the Upper House," for the "more convenient and speedier dispatch of all business." Other extracts could be given.

[1] In the recorded copies in Lib. Laws, C. and W. H., p. 106, and in Lib. W. H. and L., p. 1, it is said, the law was enacted, "with the advice and consent of the Upper and Lower House." "With the advice and consent of this general Assembly," according to the copy in Lib. No. 2. These copies seem to indicate the different stages of proceeding.

CHAPTER XIV.

Population of the Province in 1649—Predominance of the Roman Catholic Element at the Period of the Assembly—The Honor due to the Roman Catholic Freemen of Maryland.

If we take the religious elements of the population represented in this Assembly; the difference will again be in favor of the Roman Catholics.

In 1648, the burgesses appeared either as individual freemen; or as the representatives, each, of a definite number. And, in 1650, the six hundreds of St. Mary's county, as distinct integers, sent their own respective delegates. Assuming the constitution of either year, for the sake of the argument; the result, in 1649, would be substantially the same.

The settlement upon Kent Island was an offshoot of the Anglo-Catholic colony at Jamestown. Col. Clayborne was undoubtedly an Episcopalian. There, also, have we the traces of the life and labors of the Rev. Richard James, and of one or more other ministers of the Anglican church.[1] It is but just to admit, that most of the Islanders were Protestants. But the population of Kent was small. In 1639, *if not many years later*, she was but a hundred of St. Mary's county.[2] In 1648, she paid a fifth part only of the tax;[3] and did not hold, in the Assembly of that year, a larger ratio of political power.[4] That also was before the

[1] Thanks to the zeal and learned diligence of the Rev. Mr. Allen, but especially of Mr. Streeter.

[2] In 1639, was also erected the "hundred Court of Kent." Bozman, vol. 2, p. 140.

[3] From the Bill of Common Charges at the Assembly of 1648, I take, as an illustration, "The Clerk's Fees." This item amounts to 1250 pounds of tobacco, of which "Kent is to pay 250." Lib. No. 2, pp. 302–303.

[4] It was about a fifth, as the following Protest of that year will show. It is signed by all the members, including Captain Vaughan, the delegate from Kent; and Captain Bradnox, and Mr. Conner, the two freemen from that county:—

The Protest of 1648, *New Style.*

"We, the freemen assembled in this present general Assembly, do hereby declare, under our hands; and generally, jointly, and unanimously protest, against the laws which are now pretended to be put in force by the last general Assembly; conceiving that they were not lawfully enacted. For that no summons issued out

return, we may suppose, of all the Roman Catholics, who had been expelled or exported from St. Mary's, by Capt. Ingle, and the other enemies of the proprietary. In 1649, she had but one delegate; while St. Mary's was represented by eight. And this year, she paid but a sixth part of the tax.[1] And for many years after, as well as before this Assembly, there is no evidence whatever of a division of the island, or the county, even into hundreds.[2] Its population did not, in 1648, exceed the fifth; nor in 1649, the sixth part of the

to all the inhabitants, whereby their appearance was required by lawful authority. Witness our hands, this 28th January, 1647.

Robert Vaughan, 24 voices.	Robt. Clarke, proxy, Geo. Akerick, 8,
Cuthbert Fenwick, 3,	Walter Peake, 22,
Robert Percy, proxy, } 15	Wm. Thompson, proxy, Capt. Price, 9,
John Medley, }	Thomas Bradnox,
Phil. Conner,	Thomas Thornborough,
Richard Banks, 24,	Edward Packer, 3,
Thomas Allen, 6,	John Wyatt, proxy, Mr. Brooke,
George Saugher, 6,	Edwd. Cotton, proxy, Barnaby Jackson, 9
Walter Waterlen, 2,	William Bretton, 4."

Lib. No. 3, pp. 293–294; and Bozman, vol. 2, pp. 323–324.

It would seem, then, that in the Assembly of 1648, there were but 27 votes for Kent, and 130 for St. Mary's.

[1] Bill of Charges for 1649, Lib. 2, p. 488.

[2] I have carefully examined the records at Chestertown; and am satisfied this county was not laid off into hundreds till many years afterwards.

whole number of free white persons in the province.[1]

In no hundred of St. Mary's county, was there a majority of Protestants, unless in St. George's. It is not altogether certain that the Protestants outnumbered the Roman Catholics, even in that hundred. The Rev. William Wilkinson, of the English church—the first permanent pastor of the

[1] The numbers and resources of the province had been greatly diminished by the contest of Col. Clayborne, by the rebellion of Capt. Ingle, and by various other causes.

Notwithstanding the destruction of so many of the records, and the lapse of so much time, it is gratifying to think that amid the twilight of the past, we have still preserved for our own generation, many of the most important lights and landmarks of history; and that the population of the province, at the period of which I am writing, may yet be ascertained with a reasonable degree of certainty. If we multiply five by the twenty-seven votes from Kent—the number which represented, in 1648, its freemen, or the heads of its families—that county will have 135 persons. The same ratio will give to St. Mary's 650. But this estimate was true of the latter county only at the beginning of that year. The month of June, there were not less than 140 tithables, or 700 persons in this county. And the return of other colonists to St. Mary's before the succeeding April, accounts for the fact, that in 1649 Kent paid but a sixth part of the tax; at which time the whole population of the province approached 900, including the 130 or 140 inhabitants upon the Isle of Kent. For the levy and assessment of 1648 upon St. Mary's, see Lib. No. 2, p. 366, and p. 369.

Anglo-Catholic faith after the landing of the Pilgrims—but whose name has never yet appeared upon any page of Maryland's history—did not arrive in St. Mary's till the year 1650. A preacher and a planter, engaged in the discharge of his ministerial functions, as well as in the trade of the province (and what right have we to censure one who seems to have been without a temporal support from his own church?); living also, for a long period, in St. George's hundred; we cannot suppose he was altogether unsuccessful in his official labors. But even before his arrival, we there discover the germs of an early Anglican faith. In that hundred, as early as 1642, lived the Wickliffes, the Cadgers, the Marshalls, and other Episcopalians.[1] There also was the earliest home,

[1] "Council Proceedings," Lib. 1637 to 1658, pp. 203–215. Wm. Marshall's deed for "three heifers" is an interesting paper; and one of the earliest gifts upon the Records of Maryland for the support of a Protestant ministry—the very first I remember, in which allusion is made to a "parish." It may be found in Lib. No. 1, on pp. 608–609, and is dated "the 3 day of June," 1654—the proposed field of labor being a locality then called "The Neck of Wicocomico." Robt. Cadger, whose devise is mentioned by Bacon, was the only son of the Robert who came from the Old World, and who lived in St. George's in 1642. The will of the

though at a period subsequent to 1649, of the Addisons, of Oxon-Hill, a family which, for more than six generations, has borne a willing testimony to the faith of Cranmer, of Ridley, and of Latimer.[1] Conceding, what must remain a matter of considerable doubt, that St. George's was a Protestant hundred as early as 1649; and adding the county of Kent, on the eastern shore; the Protestants would hold two-sixths, or one-third, of the whole political power, substantially, if not formally, represented during this year, in the Lower House of the Assembly—an estimate which also accords with the ratio of the Protestant to the Roman

emigrant contains a conditional devise for the erecting and "maintaining of a free-school" upon his home plantation, and is dated in the year 1667. We are also struck with the fact that the person selected by the "Protestant Catholics," as the organ of their petition against Doct. Gerrard, for seizing the "key" to the chapel (see Bozman, Vol. 2, anno 1642, p. 199), resided in this very hundred; and that he bore the surname of Wickliffe, the morning-star, in the opinion of our Protestant historians, to the Reformation of the sixteenth century; certainly as important an agent in the production of that event as the great Wesley in the reproduction of the Oxford theology of the present age.

[1] In this hundred lived also Col. Price; and (I have reason to think), for a short period, Capt. Banks. But I cannot say what time they became residents.

Catholic delegates—assuming that Mr. Browne was one of the former. But it is not improbable that the Protestants constituted a fourth only of the population of Maryland.

The Protestants had, it is true, a majority in the Assembly of 1650.[1] But it was proper *that the opportunity should be offered them*, under the most favorable circumstances, of acknowledging their gratitude for so beneficent an administration of the government;[2] and of testifying in the most formal manner, that, under the proprietary's rule, they were in the enjoyment of a real, practical free-

[1] The eleven delegates from St. Mary's were John Hatch, Walter Beane, Wm. Brough, Robt. Robins, Francis Poesy, Thos. Steerman, Cuthbert Fenwick, Geo. Manners, John Medley, Philip Land, and Francis Brooke—the first six Protestants, the remaining five Roman Catholics. James Cox and Geo. Puddington (Protestants) represented the newly-erected Puritan county of Anne Arundel; while Capt. Vaughan (another Protestant) was the representative from Kent, but sat also in the Upper House. Of the hundred of St. Mary's, Messrs. Hatch and Beane represented St. George's; Messrs. Medley, Brough, and Robins, Newtown; Mr Poesy, St. Clement's; Messrs. Land and Brooke, St. Mary's; Mr. Fenwick, St. Inigoe's; and Messrs. Steerman and Manners, St. Michael's. Lib. No. 3, 47–55. See also ante, p. 71, and p. 132.

[2] This they did in a most handsome manner. See Act of Recognition in Bacon and in Bozman.

dom.[1] Even on that occasion, they outnumbered the Roman Catholic delegates from St. Mary's, by a majority of one only.[2] And it is but necessary to add, while one of the most prominent Roman Catholic delegates of 1649 was elected to the honorable post of clerk of the Assembly in 1650, and two others held a seat in that body, not a single Protestant of the latter year had represented the county in the Legislature of the former.

St. Mary's was the home—the chosen home—of the disciples of the Roman church. The fact has been generally received. It is sustained by the tradition of two hundred years, and by volumes of written testimony; by the records of the courts; by the proceedings of the privy council; by the trial of law-cases; by the wills and inventories; by the land-records, and rent-rolls; and by the very names originally given to the towns and hundreds; to the creeks and rivulets; to the tracts and manors of the county. The State itself bears the

[1] See the Protestant Declaration.

[2] The Declaration itself is quite sufficient. But abundant evidence of the fact is elsewhere preserved.

name[1] of a Roman Catholic queen.[2] Of the six hundreds of this small county, in 1650, five had the prefix of *St.* Sixty tracts and manors, most of them taken up at a very early period, bear the same Roman Catholic mark.[3] The villages and

[1] It was once very often written "Marie-Land;" and St Mary's, not unfrequently "Saint Marie's." "Terra-Mariæ" is the name given to the province in the Latin Charter.

[2] Henrietta Mariah, the wife of Charles the First, and daughter of Henry the Fourth, the great king of France—a name given also to a daughter of Capt. Neale (a favorite of the Crown), through whom the Lloyds, the Tilghmans, and many of the other most distinguished Protestant families of the province, derived the best Roman Catholic blood. The name itself has come down through the same channel, consecrated by the recollections and traditions of many generations; cherished in the memory, and enshrined in the heart of more than one living descendant of the Neales.

[3] I have easily counted this number; and am satisfied they are not all—to say nothing of many more taken up in Charles, by colonists living there in 1649, and before that county was carved out of St. Mary's. It is, of course, not certain that every one was surveyed for a Roman Catholic; nor have many of the well-known Roman Catholic estates any prefix. But who can doubt the historical value of such general evidence in estimating numbers or masses, or deny that "St. Peter's Key," "St. Peter's Hill," or most of the other tracts of this class were taken up by the members of the Roman Catholic Church? See Rent Roll for St. Mary's and Charles, Vol. 1 and 2. In the county of Anne Arundel,

creeks, to this day, attest the wide-spread prevalence of the same tastes, sentiments, and sympathies. Not long after the passage of the "Act" relating to "religion," the Protestants, it is admitted, outgrew their Roman Catholic brethren; and, in 1689, succeeded very easily in their attempt to overthrow the proprietary. But judging from the composition of the juries, in 1655, we see no reason to believe they then had a majority. In the trial of the *Piscataway* Indians,[1] during the year

the original seat of the Puritans (but soon after the home of the Quakers and of other Protestants), and at the date of the Rent Roll I have consulted, several times the area of St. Mary's, there were but three estates with the prefix! And each of these, it appears, was taken up by gentlemen, who from evidence *aliunde*, were Roman Catholics.

[1] *Skigh-tam-mough* and *Couna-weza*. They were tried at the September Term of the Provincial Court, at St. Mary's, for the murder of two negro servants. Gov. Stone, the Chief Justice, presided; the Attorney-General, Mr. Hatton, conducted the prosecution; and Mr. Fenwick was the foreman of the Jury. The scene of the murder was near South River; and the servants, as well as the plantation where the deed was done, belonged to Capt. Daniel Gookins—a name distinguished in the early history of New England. Mary, the servant, who had escaped, notwithstanding the severity of her wound, was the chief witness. But *Warcosse*, the Emperor, had sent down to St. Mary's some articles found in the possession of the suspected Indians, and which, it

1653—a case where religious bias, we may suppose, could exert but little influence on the selection of the jurors—it would be safe to assert, that, at least, twelve (or one-half of the panel) were Roman Catholics.[1] In the cases of Robert Holt,

was known, had belonged to Capt. Gookins. And the Indians, who spoke through interpreters, confessed at the trial they were present at the murder--at one moment admitting, at the next denying their guilt: "fearful, and desiring," says the record, "to conceal" it. They were convicted, sentenced, and executed on the same day. For the trial of the case, see Lib. No. 1, pp. 482–485.

[1] The Jurors were Cuthbert Fenwick, Wm. Bretton, Edward Packer, Philip Land, Wm. Evans, Richard Hoskins, Wm. Johnson, John Medley, Richard Willan, Henry Adams, James Langworth, John Thimblebee, Nicholas Gwyther, John Steerman, Richard Banks, John Lawson, Robt. Cadger, John Nichols, Daniel Clocker, Wm. Edwine, John Taylor, John Harwood, Zachary Wade, and Thomas Sympson. There is strong reason for the opinion, that the first twelve were Roman Catholics; and that eight of the other twelve were Protestants: *i.e.* Messrs. John Steerman, Richard Banks, John Lawson, Robt. Cadger, John Nichols, Daniel Clocker, Wm. Edwine, and John Taylor. The faith of the remaining four is a matter of doubt. See Appendix, No. 3. This trial, we also know, occurred after the arrival of the Puritans, and the influx of other Protestant population. The Roman Catholic, therefore, was comparatively a weaker element, in September, 1653, than in the month of April, 1649. But even then it was probably stronger than the whole combination of the Episcopal with the Puritan, and other Protestant elements. There cannot be a doubt,

and the Rev. Wm. Wilkinson,[1] in 1659, evidence of the strongest character appears. For the trial

so far as regards St. Mary's County—the only one involved in the main point of the inquiry.

[1] Indicted, the one for "bigamy;" the other as an "accessary." See Lib. S. 1658 to 1662, Judgments, pp. 200–201. They were indicted separately; but it was proposed to try them before the same jury. And they both lived in St. George's. See Indictment. Mr. Thomas Hynson, the ancestor of the Hynsons of Chestertown, was the foreman of the Grand Jury; and Mr. Thos. Ringgold, from whom so many gentlemen of the same county, and elsewhere, have derived their intermediate ancestry, was the foreman of the trial Jury. The cases are extraordinary; and the degree of Mr. Wilkinson's sin presents a difficult question for the casuist. Holt is indicted for marrying Christiana Bonnefield during the life-time of his "lawful wife;" and Parson Wilkinson for feloniously joining the parties, "after he had divorced ye said Robert Holt." The reverend gentleman "saith, that he did join" them "in marriage;" "but denyeth yt he did any thing by way of divorce;" "notwithstanding confesseth yt he drew, and signed as a witness," the paper containing "a release of all claim of marriage" "to the said Robert;" upon a confession, from the wife, of two distinct deeds of infidelity; and her subsequent "refusal to be reconciled." There is no doubt of the fact, that the parson violated the civil law. But how far he was guilty, in a religious sense (upon proof, if any, of the wife's bad faith), would depend, not only upon the soundness of the Roman Catholic theory, which elevates monogamy to the dignity of a sacrament, but also upon the condition of parties living in a sort of wilderness—the Bishop of London having no power, under the laws of England, to dissolve the bond—the Parliament, without any practical or real jurisdiction over the case—the Provincial

of these cases, twelve fit Protestants could not be found at the provincial court[1] held at St. Mary's, and usually thronged at that period with crowds of appellants and appellees; with witnesses in civil and in criminal proceedings; with spectators, and many other residents of the province![2] Immediately

Assembly never granting a divorce *a vinculo* for any cause whatever—and the English Church having no higher representative, or depositary of her authority, in this province, than the clergyman indicted. I am quite sure the legislature did not grant divorces at that time. I have no recollection, indeed, at this moment, of a single case under either of the first two proprietaries, during the sixty years before the removal of the government to Annapolis. And I do not see how Lord Baltimore, consistently with his faith in the Church of Rome, could appprove of the dissolution of a marriage.

[1] The fondness for law-suits, mingled with a veneration for judicial authority, was a striking characteristic of our ancestors. The most trifling disputes were submitted to the magistrates of the county, and afterwards to the Appellate Court of the province. St. Mary's, where the Court sat, was the great place of resort; the centre of news; and the scene of the most important business transactions.

[2] The jurors summoned for the trial were Mr. Thomas Ringgold, Robert Cadger, Nicholas Young, Daniel Clocker, William Hewes, Thomas Cadger, James Veitch, Thomas South, John Hamilton, Thomas Belcher, Robert Blunkhome, and Hugh Bemin. After the reading of the indictment, "the prisoners allege, y[t] this jury " is a very weak jury to go upon so weighty a business (they being " so nearly concerned therein) as life and death. And there being

afterwards a verdict, in another case,[1] was given by a jury taken, apparently, from the by-standers, and consisting of not less than six Roman Catholics, nor more than two Protestants[2] (one, if not both, non-residents of St. Mary's county), exclusive of the four, who had been summoned in the cases of Messrs. Holt and Wilkinson.

"few others present in court but what are Catholics, which the "prisoners afore requested might not be warned on the jury, desir-"ing that a Protestant jury might pass on them, and which the "governor consented unto, as most reasonable" (see pp. 200–201); "bail" is therefore ordered for their appearance at the next term, the governor himself becoming Mr. Wilkinson's security. But a few days later, a proclamation was issued in favor of Richard, the son of the Lord Protector, including a pardon of all persons indicted or convicted. P. 215.

[1] The case Overzee vs. Cornwallis.

[2] The jurors in this case, it would seem, were summoned upon the spur of the moment, and without the least difficulty. The Roman Catholic jurors (their faith could easily be proved by the testamentary and other records) were James Lindsey, James Langworth, Henry Adams, Richard Will, Philip Land, and a sixth, whose name I do not this moment remember; the four taken from the panel in Holt's case (all Protestants) were Thomas Ringgold, Thomas South (both, I think, residents of Kent), Thomas Belcher, and James Veitch; and the remaining two were Mr. Thomas Hynson, and Capt. Sampson Waring. See p. 201. We might also take, at randon, a jury, on p. 188; and from various records conclusively show, that one-half, if not more of them, were members of the church of Rome.

But the wills furnish the best clew to the faith of our early ancestors—precious memorials of the past—ripe harvest-fields of rich historical lore—giving us the best glimpse of our primitive life and manners—and bringing us into close and living sympathy with the state of society, two hundred years ago. But more beautiful are they than precious. For they touch our hearts. They breathe the spirit of parental affection, in all its depth and wild intensity. They point from the rude home, where the weary pilgrim of the forest lies down to die in his humility, to a bright and everlasting mansion prepared for him in the skies! This day, they speak—voices from the dead—a willing testimony to a mighty truth in the history of a continent, and to a sublime doctrine of the Christian religion! More of them emanate from a Roman Catholic than from a Protestant source. The will of William Smith, one of the original pilgrims of 1634, appears upon the first page of the oldest testamentory record at Annapolis; and contains the living evidence of his faith in the church of Rome. It would be difficult to give all the recorded confessions, or the half of those little testimonials of love and fidelity, which were bequeathed to the same church, during the fifty years succeeding the settlement at St. Mary's. But it will be sufficient to say, the Roman Catholic greatly exceed the number of Protestant wills;[1] and of the latter (or those having any sort of anti-Roman-Catholic mark), many are signed by the Quakers—a denomination, of whom there is no trace upon the provincial records, as early as 1649.

Counting the suitors and freeholders of the different manors, with all the indented white servants, it is highly probable, that every hundred of St. Mary's county, except St. George's, had a majority of Roman Catholics, in 1649. Excluding the servants (a large class, at that time), there can be little doubt upon the point of mere numbers, and

[1] I have examined most of the wills anterior to 1650, including those from Kent Island. And as far as any result may be based upon so general an inquiry, I find the Roman Catholic (or those either having upon their face a Roman Catholic mark, or known from other evidence to have been signed by Roman Catholics) bear to the Protestant wills in both counties, a ratio of not less than *four to one*. Messrs. Fenwick and Manners are the only burgesses of the Assembly in 1649, whose wills are preserved. It is not unworthy of note, that both papers are strongly marked Roman Catholic ones.

none whatever with regard to superior influence. Even, in 1650, St. Mary's hundred was represented by two disciples of the Roman church; and there also was the seat of the proprietary's government. In St. Michael's, were the three manors of Governor Leonard Calvert, to say nothing of other evidence. Doctor Thomas Gerard was the lord of two large manors, in St. Clement's; and Newtown had more estates with the prefix of *St.*[1] than any hundred erected before or after the year 1649. St. Inigo's was probably not carved out either of St. Mary's, or of St. Michael's, before the year 1650; but included a manor held by the missionaries as early as 1639,[2] with the manor-house,[3] or supposed seat of one of the interesting little Roman Catholic missions.

Nor ought the activity of many of the priests, in converting the Protestants; or the large number of emigrants they also had introduced;[4] be omit-

[1] Rent Roll for St. Mary's and Charles, vol. 1, Newtown hun dred.

[2] See Rent Roll, St. Inigo's manor.

[3] St. Inigo's House was the residence of Father Copley. See Lib. No. 1, pp. 212–13, and p. 500.

[4] They transported (see Governor Green's testimony, Lib. No.

ted in this outline of the evidence. For some of the methods they adopted in the propagation of their faith, writers of a different church have censured them. But the very reproach implies a concession. Before the year 1649, they labored with their lay-assistants, in various fields;[1] and around their lives will for ever glow a bright and glorious remembrance. Their pathway was through the desert; and their first chapel, the *wigwam* of an Indian.[2] Two of them were here, at the dawn of

1, p. 166) not less than sixty persons—most of them, we may presume, Roman Catholics, either before or after their arrival.

[1] We have no complete catalogue of the Roman Catholic Missionaries, who arrived before the year 1649. But the following embraces nearly all: The Reverend Messrs. Andrew White (styled not untruly "The Apostle of Maryland"); John Altham; a third not named, in 1635; Thomas Copley; Ferdinando Pulton; Father Ferret, the year of whose arrival is involved in doubt; John Brock, whose real paternal name, it is said, was Morgan; Philip Fisher, and Roger Rigbie. John Knoles, Thomas Gervass, and Mr. Morley, were three of the temporal coadjutors, or lay-brothers. The Rev. Lawrence Starkie, another Jesuit Missionary, came soon after the Assembly of 1649; probably about the time of Parson Wilkinson's arrival.

[2] I speak, not figuratively, but in a strictly historical sense. Obtaining the consent of the aboriginal occupant, they fitted up the little hut, the best manner their means would allow, and called it "The First Chapel in Maryland." See Campbell.

our history:[1] they came to St. Mary's with the original emigrants; they assisted, by pious rites, in laying the corner-stone of a State; they kindled the torch of civilization in the wilderness; they gave consolation to the grief-stricken pilgrim; they taught the religion of CHRIST to the simple sons of the forest. The history of Maryland presents no better, no purer, no more sublime lesson than the story of the toils, sacrifices, and successes of her early missionaries.[2]

Looking, then, at the question, under both of its aspects—regarding the faith, either of the delegates, or of those whom they substantially represented—we cannot but award the chief honor to the members of the Roman church. To the Roman Catholic freemen of Maryland, is justly

[1] The Jesuit Fathers, who came in 1634, were the Rev. Messrs. White and Altham. The same year, also, arrived John Knoles, and Thomas Gervass. See Campbell's Missions, and McSherry's Maryland.

[2] Honor to the memory of the Rev. Mr. McSherry, and of Col. Barney U. Campbell, for their labors in this department of our history. Maryland owes a debt of gratitude; while the lovers of learning, in other States, will not fail to cherish a grateful estimate of their contributions to our literature.

due the main credit arising from the establishment, by a solemn legislative act, of religious freedom for all believers in Christianity.

CHAPTER XV.

Cecilius, the Lord Proprietary. His Life, Character, and Family.

If the founders of our political liberty—if the signers of the Declaration of Independence—now receive the admiration and the homage of the civilized world; the early law-givers of Maryland—the originators of our religious freedom—have clearly a right to some place upon the page of American history.

Happily for the present generation, something is yet known, not only of the proprietary and the first governor, but also of almost every member of the Assembly, in 1649.

The Calverts of England derived their descent from a Flemish noble family. Their armorial bearings are traced to a very remote period; but the meritorious services, for which they were granted, or the honorable deeds they commemorated, cannot now be fully ascertained. They are: *paly of six, or and sable, a bend counterchanged;*

and were engraved upon the early seal of the province,[1] occupying the first and fourth quarters of the escutcheon. They are also borne by the English Calverts now living at Albury Hall, and at Hunsdon in Herts.[2] And they reappear, after the lapse of many years, upon the present seal of the State. George, the father of Cecilius, was born in Yorkshire, about the year 1582. He represented that county in the Parliament in 1620; and Oxford at a later period. He held, at various times, the posts of private secretary to Sir Robert Cecil; clerk to the privy council; and one of the secretaries of state. In 1617 he was knighted;[3] and about 1625 created Baron of Baltimore. He was a member of the Virginia Company, in 1609; and at a much later period, received the charter for a part of

[1] According to Lord Baltimore's instruction (see the Commission for the Great Seal, Bosman, vol. 2, p. 652), six pieces were requisite. But upon the provincial Seal, there were, in point of fact, but five—the result, I presume of the engraver's mistake or carelessness—and a defect, I find, perpetuated by our new Seal, which follows the provincial too closely in that, but not enough so, it strikes me, in some other particulars—an opinion submitted with unaffected diffidence.

[2] Burke's Dictionary of the Landed Gentry.

[3] Kennedy's First Lord Baltimore.

Newfoundland, where he attempted to plant a colony. Disheartened with the enterprise, he went to Virginia; but finding he was there required to take an oath inconsistent with his fidelity to the church of Rome, he returned to England, after a survey of the country bordering upon the Chesapeake; and shortly before his death, obtained the promise of a charter for the province of Maryland, and which was given to his son.

Cecilius had imbibed the spirit of his father. And faithfully did he carry out the noble design. The respect which is due to his memory, arises not only from the part he performed in laying the foundations of religious liberty; but also from the liberal policy he adopted, in the establishment and government of the colony in every other particular. During the first few years, he expended upwards of forty thousand pounds sterling—a very large sum at that time. The lands he granted to the emigrants upon easy conditions, and at a rent almost nominal.[1] And, although he manifested no sympathy with republicanism, in its present sense (the supposition betrays, indeed, a

[1] Kilty's Landholder's Assistant, pp. 29–45.

great aosurdity), the whole administration was distinguished for its mild, and just, its beneficent, and paternal character. Tradition, also, has given him the appellation of Pater Patriæ. And the journal of the Assembly,[1] the proceedings of the courts, the frequent acts of executive clemency, and the admissions even of Protestants, are full of the strongest and most interesting testimony. As the patron of the early Roman Catholic missions, he also has a claim upon our regards. Could anything have been conceived in the spirit of a more sublime charity? Singular, also, was the sense of justice, which marked his conduct in everything relating to the aborigines. The Indians looked up to him as their patriarch. The chiefs upon the Piscataway, and upon other streams, were accustomed to submit their gravest questions to the decision of his government. To them, as well as to the colonists, was he indeed a guardian; tempering justice with mercy in every case compatible with the principles of order, and with the great ends of civil society. "Halcyon"[2] was the period;

[1] McMahon's Maryland.

[2] A word used by many Protestants, soon after the overthrow

and happy the people. Unfortunately for his memory, no artist has yet arisen to do him historical justice. The scene at *Yaocomico*,[1] upon the landing of the Maryland pilgrims, is not unworthy of the pencil of a West; and the other treaties of of Lord Baltimore with the Indians, do not lack the dignity of the one signed at *Shakamaxon*,[2] and which has given such wide celebrity to the venerable name of Penn.

It is painful to think of the case of Col. Clayborne. His heroism was unquestionable; and his motive in founding a colony upon an island of the Chesapeake, was of the most honorable character. His fate was hard; and history has done injustice to his memory. The friends of historical learning are indebted to the late labors of a gentleman now living at Baltimore;[3] and for the light he has shed upon the controversy, I also am under much obli-

of the proprietary's government, in 1689; and applicable to the days of Cecilius as well as to those of Charles.

[1] Subsequently St. Mary's. The Proprietary, it is needless to add, was not personally present; but the spirit of his policy was fairly represented by his brother, Gov. Calvert.

[2] Where a part of Philadelphia now stands.

[3] Mr. S. F. Streeter.

gation. It seems the principle upon which the founder of the Kent Island settlement had based his claim, was not without some support, in a clause of the Maryland charter.[1] It appears, also, with great force, in the case of the early Dutch and Swedish settlements upon the Delaware; and in the one decided about a century later, it is indirectly sanctioned, so far as regards the ground of prior occupancy, by the celebrated opinion of an English chancellor.[2] But Clayborne, unlike Penn, never had a charter. The contest in Maryland was bitter and bloody. Both settlements had suffered much misery and loss. And upon Clayborne's own appeal to the authorities of the English government, the course of the proprietary upon the main point, was sustained. The claimant from Virginia committed another error. He con-

[1] Clayborne founded his settlement before the arrival of the Pilgrims at St. Mary's, or even the date of Lord Baltimore's charter, which did not, in clear language, include any colonized territory. The claim of the Swedes upon the Delaware also embraced within the Maryland charter (as far up as the fortieth degree including the site of Philadelphia), was partly based upon the same ground as that of Clayborne.

[2] Lord Hardwick. See Reports, 1 Vesey, Sr., pp. 444–456. This decision virtually settled the long and tedious controversy between Maryland and Pennsylvania.

founded the question of jurisdiction with the right to the soil; and Maryland could not consent to the exercise by Virginia of any sovereignty over the Isle of Kent. Nor was Clayborne, as the occupant of land there, justified in retaining his allegiance to the government at Jamestown. At the origin of his settlement, our sister colony, it will be remembered, existed by the sufferance, or at best by the guardianship of the English crown.[1] And there is no evidence whatever of the proprietary's unwillingness at the beginning of the controversy, to grant, upon the proper application, a full confirmation of the title to every tract the secretary of Virginia had reclaimed from the wilderness. The purchase from the Indians was not sufficient.[2]

Cecilius died in 1675. As early, however, as 1662, he sent Charles, his son and heir, who lived

[1] It has been said, the charter to Lord Baltimore for territory within the original limits of Virginia invaded the rights of that colony. But the one given to Virginia was taken away, however unjustly, before the date of Lord Baltimore's.

[2] It was against a well established principle in the policy of nations, to recognize a title, without a previous sanction from the Crown, of which the purchaser was a subject. Such is also the law of the United States.

many years in the province, a part of the time at Mattapany-Sewall;[1] sharing the fortunes of the other colonists; and marrying the widow[2] of one of the most distinguished; giving evidence of those noble qualities, which had rendered the memory of the first proprietary so dear to the people of Maryland; and amid many embarrassments, leaving, both as a governor and a proprietary, the indelible foot-prints of an able, a wise, and a just administration. From Charles is traced the descent of the other proprietaries[3] now represented by the Cal-

[1] Near the mouth of the Patuxent, originally the dwelling-place the *Mattapanients* (one of the most friendly tribes of Maryland); next, the storehouse of the Jesuit Missions; but subsequently relinquished by the Missionaries; and given by the Proprietary to the Hon. Henry Sewall, the privy councillor. The Mansion during Lord Charles Baltimore's residence, was the Government House of the Province. There, also, once stood a fort and a magazine.

[2] Jane, the widow of the Honorable Henry Sewall, the privy councillor, and the ancestor of the Sewalls of Mattapany-Sewall, including the descendants at Poplar-Hill, Prince George's County.

[3] The errors of Lodge (see his "Irish Peerage") were perpetuated by the "London Magazine" of June 1768; and some of the members of the family, at this time, are under the impression that John, instead of Charles, was the third baron of Baltimore. The following statement consists of facts derived from the provincial records, from the State Law Reports, and from other sources of

8

verts of Prince George's County—George and his brothers being the grandsons of Benedict, the son of the fifth baron,[1] and who bore the baton in his escutcheon. Mount Airy, in the same county, has been the family seat, for several generations. May it long remain the home of the Calverts![2]

the most reliable character. George was the first baron; Cecilius the second baron and the first lord proprietary; Charles I. the third baron and second proprietary; Benedict Leonard, the fourth baron and third proprietary; Charles II., the fifth baron and fourth proprietary; and Frederick, the fifth proprietary; at whose death, for want of legal issue, the barony became extinct; but he gave the lord-proprietaryship to his natural son, Henry Harford, a highly accomplished gentleman, and whose authority, at the period of the American Revolution, was represented by Governor Robert Eden.

[1] There is also a branch at Riversdale, near Washington; and another at Newport, R. I.; both offshoots from Mount Airy.

[2] Nelly, the daughter of Benedict, was married to Mr. Custis. The letter of General Washington, the guardian of the gentleman who had sought her hand, is published in Sparks's Collection, vol. 2, p. 371.

CHAPTER XVI.

Governor Leonard Calvert.

The planting of a colony, amid the dangers and privations of a wilderness, from the most ancient to a comparatively modern period, assumed a high rank among the "heroical works"[1] of man. In the history of Maryland, we see the union of the hero with the pilgrim; the combination of a mission derived from the laws of human destiny, and expressly given before the Fall, with the magnificent and sublime sentiment, which soon became a living embodiment, under the form of religious liberty. The first of the spirits who personally took part in the noble adventure, and the chief of the original pilgrims, was Gov. Leonard Calvert.[2] The brother of the proprietary—young, but dis-

[1] Lord Bacon.

[2] He also bore the baton in his escutcheon. See Hildreth, Vol. I. p. 209.

creet; full of confidence in his own strength, yet fondly relying upon a higher power; devoting his life and fortunes, in the most energetic and honorable manner, to the task of guiding and protecting the little band of emigrants—he seems to have presented a practical exemplification of that beautiful conception, which pervades the bosom of the idealist in every age; representing the ruler of a grateful people, under the striking similitude of a shepherd. The visions of childhood are dispelled by the sober sense of manhood. But youth is the type of a cheerful spirit, and of a hopeful heart—the season of daring enterprise, and of heroic adventure. At the darkest hour in the fortunes of the colony, the soul of young Calvert never despaired. Once driven from the capital by the enemies of the proprietary; he rallied a force in Virginia; and returning to Maryland, at a propitious moment, recovered the government, which had been wrested from his grasp by the hand of pirates and traitors. The proprietary, of a less sanguine temperament, had regarded the temporary success of Ingle's arms in Maryland, with other untoward events, as a knell to the hopes of his colony; and accordingly instructed Governor Calvert to gather up the wreck of his private property; apparently abandoning for ever his rights under the charter.[1] But the courage of Calvert was not subdued; his energy, at the most trying crisis, was not wanting. Pledging the personal resources of the proprietary, and making another effort, he succeeded. To him is due the honor of re-establishing the government, against the most fearful odds; and of securing the field, which had been lost, for a fair experiment of those principles of religious liberty, which have since become the pride and boast of Maryland. Although his death occurred before the year 1649, he occupies a high and honorable place among the law-reformers of his age—having exhibited the first practical example of toleration, in his twofold character of governor and chief justice—in the former, exerting the largest discretionary power, both under the charter, and also under his commission from the proprietary—in the latter, anticipating the statute law, and shaping the judicial policy of the province, in a manner which reflected the liberal spirit of Cecilius. His tomb-

[1] McSherry.

stone cannot be found; and our ignorance of the spot is a reproach to the living generation of Marylanders. But he was "a great and good man," more illustrious for what he founded than the most successful generals for what they have overthrown and destroyed.[1] The sincerity of his faith in the Church of Rome has never been questioned.[2]

[1] McSherry.

[2] I have no knowledge of his posterity; and doubt if he was ever married.

CHAPTER XVII.

Governor William Stone.

THE ancestors of Gov. William Stone probably resided in Northamptonshire, in England.[1] But he had one, if not several kinsmen[2] at London.

[1] His earliest American residence of which I have any recorded knowledge, was in Northampton County, Va.; Nanjemy River, upon which stood his manor, in Charles county, Md., bore, about the time of the original survey, the name (Lib. No. 12, p. 116) of Avon; and Mr. Thos. Sprigg, of Prince George's county, whom in his will (Lib. No. 1, 1635 to 1674, p. 90) he calls "brother," held a tract (Liber, Wills, T. B., No. 2, p. 444) also named Northampton I am inclined to think, the governor gave the name to Northampton county.

[2] He had (Lib. No. 2, pp. 313, 314) a near relation at London, whose very street is given, and whose name was Thomas; and one of the divisions of Nanjemy Manor (called also the Manor of Poynton) was bounded (Lib. No. 11, p. 330) by Cheapside creek. He had at least two brothers. John also probably lived at London; Mathew, in the province of Maryland. And several families of his surname, with distinct armorial bearings, resided at that city. With the aid derived from these facts, especially by connecting Thomas with the street he lived upon, it would be easy, it strikes me, to obtain the further evidence which is no doubt preserved

And we may suppose he came from that city to America. He was the high sheriff in one of the counties of Virginia, before he received his commission from Lord Baltimore. The early part of 1649, he arrived in Maryland; and the same year, brought six persons into the province.[1] It seems also he took a kind and active part in securing a home for the Puritans from Virginia.[2] At the Assembly of 1649, he presided over the privy councillors, when they sat separately from the burgesses; and over both branches when the members assembled in one body. In 1652, his unhappy contest began with the Puritan party.[3] The Eng-

upon the records there, and thus to establish the identity of his with one of the other families; as well as to ascertain his own arms. For the armorial bearings of the different families of Stone, see Burke's General Armory.

[1] Lib. No. 2, p. 425.

[2] Such is the opinion of a very respectable authority. It is also certain (see his commission for the office of governor, in Bozman) that he had undertaken to introduce 500 persons. But I have never seen the proof of the fulfilment of his engagement, nor the reasons of his failure.

[3] Many of the facts of this sketch not directly taken from the Records, will be found in Bozman's Maryland, to which I must refer my readers for a long but interesting, and in most respects strictly accurate account of the controversy.

lish parliament had sent out commissioners, with instructions to bring under subjection the colonies upon the Chesapeake; and the governor was ready to acknowledge the authority of the home government, as it had been organized without a king or a house of lords. But more was exacted. And changes rapidly succeeded each other, not without violence, and greatly to the distress and disturbance of the whole province. Acting under instructions from the proprietary, and aiming to re-establish the form of government recognized by the charter, he marched from St. Mary's, in 1655, at the head of a little army; and near the site of Annapolis was fought a memorable battle,[1] in which the Puritans exhibited much fanaticism, great bravery, and extreme brutality. The governor "received a wound in his shoulder;" and most of his surviving adherents, including Col. Price, surrendered. The victorious party then held a court-martial; passed sentence upon many; exe-

[1] The battlefield, it is supposed, was at the site of Fort Horn, nearly opposite Greenberry's Point, where stood the first Puritan town. See Leonard Strong's "Babylon's Fall," and Langford's "Refutation," Ridgely's "Annals," and other authorities. In another note, I have noticed the origin of the town.

cuted several; and, in cold blood, shot William Eltonhead, a privy councillor, a Roman Catholic, and a near relation of Mr. Fenwick. Through the earnest intercession of some of their own soldiers, the governor was rescued from the fate of Charles the First! The estates of the prisoners were next sequestered; heavy and cruel fines inflicted. And the governor was one of the greatest sufferers, through the agency of the very men whom, but a few years before, we have good reason for believing, he had so generously befriended. Some time after the restoration of the proprietary's government, he was a privy councillor; and, throughout his whole life, sustained a high reputation for integrity and honor. Soon after his arrival, he lived in St. Michael's hundred; the latter part of his life, upon "Poynton Manor," then called Nanjemy; a part of which had been granted, in consideration of his "good and faithful services."[1] At his death, which occurred about 1660, he had a house also at

[1] Lib. Q. pp. 179–180. The original patent embraced 5000 acres; and was held of the "honor of West St. Mary's;" with the usual powers and privileges of a manor, including that of holding the court-leet and the court-baron.

St. Mary's city. He left many children;[1] whose posterity also resided upon the Manor. And most of his descendants, like himself,[2] were Protestants; including the Rt. Rev. William Murray Stone,[3] the third bishop in the Protestant Episcopal succession of Maryland. Many also of his descendants are distinguished in the civil and military annals of our country—Thomas,[4] his great-great-grandson, having signed the Declaration of American Independence; Michael Jenifer, the brother of Thomas, having

[1] Verlinda was his wife; and Thomas, Richard, Elizabeth, John, Mathew, Catharine, and Mary, were some of his children. See his will (Lib. No. 1, 1635 to 1674, pp. 90–93),) where he names also his brother-in-law, Francis Doughty; and Richard, the uncle of his son, Richard Stone.

[2] See Signers of the Protestant Declaration.

[3] Of the eastern-shore branch, quite remote from the present representatives in Charles. But the relationship was claimed and recognized as late as the life-time of the bishop.

[4] Thomas, the granduncle of Frederick, it is well known, was the son of David, who died about 1772. And it can be proved from the testamentary, and other records, that David was the son of Thomas, and the grandson of John, the son of the provincial governor. The principal part of the proof is derived from their wills, recorded at Annapolis, and probably at Port Tobacco. The ascent also of Thomas, the son of William, may be traced, through the grandfather, Thomas, to Governor William, the great-grandfather. See their wills.

been a member of the Convention which, in 1788, ratified the Constitution of the United States; and John, another brother, and who had been wounded at Long Island, having held the post of governor, in this State, nearly a hundred and fifty years after the date of the commission from the proprietary for the same office, to William, the emigrant. And Frederick, now living at Port Tobacco, and a descendant of the sixth degree, through Michael Jenifer, from the early provincial governor, is one of the commissioners engaged in the grave work of reforming the practice of the courts in Maryland.

CHAPTER XVIII.

Governor Thomas Green.

GOVERNOR GREEN was one of the pilgrims of 1634,[1] and the intimate friend of Governor Calvert. He was a privy councillor, as early as 1639; and for many subsequent years. The two short periods he held the post of governor are involved in too much obscurity to warrant any important inference, beyond the fact of his sincere attachment to the interests of the royal family at home.[2] Governor Calvert appointed him, upon his death-bed, simply to supply a vacancy, in 1647.[3] Under Governor Stone's appointment, he was also the chief executive, a part of 1649. Of his faith, there is no doubt. One of his children was the namesake and godson of the first governor.[4] And, in a trust-deed

[1] Lib. A. B. & H., p. 67; and Lib. No. 1, p. 41.

[2] See the proclamation in favor of Charles the Second, in 1649, Bozman, vol. 2, p. 670.

[3] Bozman, vol. 2, p. 307.

[4] See Gov. Calvert's will.

to Henry Adams and James Langworth, in 1650, he expressly says he is a Roman Catholic; and gives by the same instrument, in testimony of the fact, a token of regard for the Rev. Thomas Copley.[1] He was several times married, and lived, it would seem, a short time before his death, in Virginia. He had four sons.[2] His descendants resided in Charles County, at a period not long before the American Revolution. And some of his posterity[3] are probably now in the State. We have no reason to doubt he was present, in the Assembly, during all the important proceedings relating to the Toleration Act.

[1] Lib. No. 1, pp. 188–189.

[2] See his deed to Messrs. Adams & Langworth. Their names were Thomas, Leonard, Robert, and Francis. He had also a brother named Robert. See Lib. No. 2, p. 444.

[3] Green's Inheritance was one of the tracts held by them.

CHAPTER XIX.

Colonel John Price.

THE year of Colonel John Price's arrival is involved in doubt.[1] But in 1639,[2] he represented St. Michael's hundred in the General Assembly; and soon rose to eminence, as a soldier. His services are the subject of the proprietary's notice; and as a mark of his merit, he received the commission of mustermaster-general of the province, in 1648.[3] The same year, he was appointed a privy councillor. He was distinguished for his fidelity, during the insurrections and rebellions beginning in 1645. And perhaps to his soldier-like skill and courage, was Governor Calvert chiefly indebted for the recovery of his authority. He also had the command of St. Inigo's Fort, at a

[1] Several persons of his name came about the same time.

[2] Bozman.

[3] Bozman, vol. 2, pp. 652.

very critical period. He was a signer of the Protestant declaration in 1650; one of the chief sufferers, at an advanced stage of his life, under the misrule of the Puritans;[1] and, as a privy councillor, at a subsequent period, sat upon the bench of the Provincial Court. He died in 1661. As a soldier, a councillor, and a provincial judge, he sustained the highest character. Judging from his will, he was also a kind master. He bequeathed a token of his benevolence to each of the six indented white-servants who had lived with him.[2] He was illiterate; but nature had given him the best powers of observation and perception. His opinions in council are marked with a candor worthy of the knight; and generally, if not always, on the side of a strict conservatism;[3] short, indeed, yet full of pith, and directly to the point. Those upon the bench are equally brief; but still

[1] Lib. No. 3.

[2] "I give and bequeath," he also says, "unto my loving friend, Mr. William Wilkinson, the sum of 350 pounds of tobacco, for the preaching of my funeral sermon." His daughter was named Ann. See the Will, Lib. No. 1, 1635 to 1674, p. 141.

[3] Witness his pithy opinion against the revolutionary manœuvre of Gov. Fendall. See Council Proceedings.

distinguished for their strong and clear sense of justice. The sword, however, and not the pen, was the emblem of his greatest excellence. It was in the garrison and the field, rather than at the council-board, in the march against the Indians more than in the delivery of judicial decisions, that we find, he was conspicuous. But we have every reason to believe, the part he took in the Assembly of 1649, was in the highest degree honorable to his memory. Of the posterity of this rude and unlettered, but still genuine cavalier of St. George's hundred (for there he resided the latter part of his life), nothing is known beyond the mention of a daughter in his will.

CHAPTER XX.

Honorable John Pile.

THE Honorable John Pile[1] was probably a native of Wilts. And his residence upon the Wicomico, in Maryland, granted for "good and acceptable services," consisting of four hundred,[2] but subsequently of a thousand acres,[3] bore the name of *Salisbury*.[4] It was the home also of his posterity for several generations. Before 1648, he

[1] The appellation of "Honorable" was given at a very early period, to the members of the Privy Council, and to the Judges of the Provincial Court. The name of Mr. Pile is, in some places upon the Record, spelt *Pyle*—at others, *Pille*.

[2] Records of the Land Office, Lib. Q., pp. 447–448.

[3] Rent-Roll for St. Mary's and Charles, vol. 2, fol. 371.

[4] It is generally called "Sarum"—another name only for the old borough in Wilts, where also, about two miles distant, is the city of "New-Sarum," or Salisbury. In Liber S., 1658 to 1662, "Judgments" (see p. 221), the plantation is called "Salisbury." Salisbury was the name also of another tract held by the privy councillor's son. See Joseph's will, Testamentary Records at Annapolis, Lib. No. H., pp. 64–65.

arrived, with his wife;[1] and under his immediate care, during that year, came also the Tettershalls,[2] his relations,[3] professing the same faith,[4] and apparently from the same English county.[5] In 1649

[1] Records of the Land Office, Lib. No. 2, pp. 508–509. His wife's name is not given; but it was, no doubt, "Sarah"—the name borne by his wife, in 1660. See Records of the Court of Appeals, Lib. S., 1658 to 1662, Judgments, p. 221.

[2] Their names were William and Mary. Records of the Land Office, Lib. No. 2, pp. 508–509.

[3] The privy councillor frequently calls William Tettershall his "brother." *E.g.*, see Lib. S., 1658 to 1662, "Judgments," p. 1072. He also calls Lieut. Col. John Jarboe his "brother." Land Office Records, Lib. No. 1, p. 247.

[4] William Tettershall's Will (see Lib. No. 1, 1635 to 1674, among the Testamentary Records in the Register's Office, at Annapolis) contains incontestable evidence of the fact. He also calls Lieut. Col. Jarboe (R. Catholic) his "brother."

[5] William Tettershall (see his will) mentions his brother John, "of Oddstoake, in Wiltshire." It seems also he had two other brothers: Lawrence, who lived at the same place, in Wilts, about 1648; and Peter, who resided at "Chidooch," in Dorchester, England. See the deed of his nephew, Edmund Smith, of Maryland, to Cuthbert Fenwick, upon the Records of the Land Office, Lib. No. 2, p. 439. The Tettershalls of Maryland subsequently lived in Prince George's. The supposition, that the Piles came from Salisbury, in England, is confirmed not only by the preceding facts relating to the Tettershalls, but also by a marriage mentioned in the history of the Pophams, of Littlecott, in Wilts. About 1640, Elizabeth, the daughter of Sir Francis Popham, was married to Sir Gabriel Pile. The residence of Sir Gabriel is not

and 1650, he sat in the privy council;[1] but his commission is dated in 1648.[2] One of his descendants, it is said, became a Roman Catholic clergyman; and another a nun.[3] Of the sincerity of his own faith, we have the recorded evidence. During the ascendency of the Puritans, at the period of a bitter persecution, he comes forward; and "*confesseth himself in court to be a Roman Catholic*"—acknowledging "*the Pope's supremacy.*"[4] The time of his death is not known; nor can his will be found. But in 1660, he had three children, whose names were Joseph, Ann, and

stated. But I cannot but think he lived in the same county; and was a relation of the Piles of Maryland. See Burke's Dictionary of the Landed Gentry, vol. 2, p. 1058. Constance, the daughter of George Tattershall, of Wilts, was married to Wm. Smith. See same authority, Vol. 2, p. 1354. There is no history in that work, of the Piles of Wilts, nor of any family of the same name.

[1] See certificate prefixed to the Declaratory law of 1650, Records of the Land Office, Lib. No. 3, p. 45.

[2] Bozman, vol. 2, p. 650.

[3] The Testamentary Records also show how fondly attached were the Piles of Maryland to the faith of their forefathers. See, *e. g.*, the will of Joseph, in 1692.

[4] The following is the entry upon the Record of the Provincial Court, in the Land Office, for October Term, in 1655: "John Pyle confesseth himself, in court, to be a Roman Catholic; and hath acknowledged the Pope's supremacy." See Lib. No. 3, p. 161.

Mary.[1] His son died in 1692,[2] giving Salisbury to Joseph, the only grandson, and leaving Sarah with two other descendants. His grandson, whose will is dated in 1724, divided the family seat between the five great-grandchildren, Joseph, Bennett, Ann, Elizabeth, and Mary.[3] Of Joseph, the privy councillor's great-grandson, there is an entry upon the records, as late as 1738.[4] At his death, the family, in the male line, it is supposed, became extinct. But there are descendants through several female representatives. It is said, the blood of the privy councillor still flows through the veins of the Brents of Louisiana, the descendants of Robert Brent, of Charles County; and that it is also represented by the children of Henry J. Carroll, of St. Mary's, in Maryland.

[1] Records of the Court of Appeals, in the Armory of the State House, Lib. S. 1658 to 1662, Judgments, p. 221.

[2] Will of Joseph Pile, Lib. No. H., pp. 64–65.

[3] Will of Joseph, the grandson, Lib. W. B. No. 1, pp. 312–313. The testator also calls John Parnham his "brother."

[4] He was one of the witnesses to the will of John Parnham, dated in 1738; and in which are mentioned John, Francis, Xaverius, Ann Maria, and Elizabeth, the children of the testator, and probably the descendants of the privy councillor.

CHAPTER XXI.

Captain Robert Vaughan.

Captain Vaughan held land upon Kent Island,[1] upon Langford's Bay,[2] and upon the Chester River.[3] One of the tracts taken up by him, was called "Ruerdon," and another "Kimbolton"—the name also of a small town in Huntingdonshire, England. He was one of the Protestant members[4] of the privy council, in 1649 and 1650. In 1638, he held the office of constable[5] for St. George's hundred, in St. Mary's County—a post, at that time, not below the dignity of a gentleman. In 1642, he was one of the representatives[6] in the General Assembly, from the Isle of Kent. He

[1] Rent Roll for Talbot and Queen Anne's, vol. 2, fol. 299.
[2] Records of the Land Office, Lib. Q. p. 333.
[3] Lib. Q., p. 338.
[4] See his signature to the Protestant Declaration.
[5] Bozman, vol. 2, p. 45.
[6] Bozman, vol. 2, p. 215.

also represented the Island, during many subsequent sessions of the Legislature. In 1647, he was the commander,[1] or viceroy, of Kent. In 1648, he received two commissions[2] from the proprietary—the one investing him with the office of a privy councillor; the other re-appointing him to the post of commander. In the latter, there is a strong testimony to his "fidelity, courage," and "wisdom," during the "insurrection" of Capt. Ingle, and his accomplices. About the first of November, during the same year, he was removed from the commandership of the Island,[3] in consequence of his disrespectful language towards Governor Green; but re-instated, upon the offer of an apology. Having become involved in a dispute with the commissioners of the County Court, he asked and received their forgiveness also.[4] In 1652, complaints were expressed by the inhabitants of the Island.[5] We cannot say what they were. But he

[1] Bozman, vol. 2, p. 304. [2] Bozman, vol. 2, pp. 649 and 653.

[3] Bozman, vol. 2, p. 660–661.

[4] See Record of the County Court, at Chestertown, in the Clerk's Office, marked "Court Proceedings" (a fragment only of it remains), and beginning in the year "1647."

[5] See Bozman, vol. 2, p 453–454. But Mr. Bozman is mistaken

was soon afterwards removed from the office of commander, by Richard Bennett, and the other commissioners appointed by Governor Stone. The office he had held, somewhat analogous to that of lieutenant-general, was one of the most honorable within the limits of the province.[1] He had exercised the power of granting land-warrants; but failed to transmit a copy of his record[2]—an omission which nothing could justify, and which we can excuse[3] only, upon the supposition then preva-

in supposing Capt. Vaughan was not removed by the commissioners. See the preceding "Court Proceedings," at Chestertown, beginning in "1647." The Record does not, indeed, contain the charges or the trial. But we will find there the *order* of the commissioners displacing Capt. Vaughan.

[1] In the commission of 1648 (see Bozman, vol. 2, p. 653), he was clothed with the power of selecting his councillors; of holding courts, whenever there was a necessity; of deciding all civil cases "not exceeding" ten pounds sterling; and of disposing of all criminal ones "determined by any justice of the peace in England," in the "courts of session, not extending to life or member." Some of the early commissions conferred also a great deal of military and executive authority. See Bozman for a copy of these commissions.

[2] Bozman, vol. 2, p. 460–463.

[3] In extenuation of Capt. Vaughan's delinquency, it may be added, that the commander of Anne Arundel also failed to transmit a copy of his proceedings. And even the surveyor-general,

lent in the province, that the English government had resolved to deprive the proprietary of his lawful authority. The power to grant warrants was, therefore, revoked by Governor Stone, the latter part of 1652.[1] The date of Capt. Vaughan's death cannot be given. But he left two children: William,[2] who died in 1684; and Mary, the wife of Major James Ringgold,[3] of Huntingfield. Wil-

Robert Clarke, a Roman Catholic, did not make a due return, in 1652, of the certificates from that county, and from Kent.

[1] Bozman, vol. 2, p. 463.

[2] The will of William Vaughan is recorded in Lib. G. See p. 64. He desires his friends to bury him "near ye body of his deceased father;" requests Major Ringgold to be the "guardian" to his two little children; and gives his daughter a tract of 200 acres upon the Island, and which is still called "Parson's Point;" but does not name either of the children—speaking of them, simply, as his "son" and "daughter." He divides the rest of the estate between his wife and two children.

[3] The following is an extract (see Lib. G., pp. 232–233) from the will of Major Ringgold: "I give and bequeath unto my son, James Ringgold, the plantation I now live on, provided that my son, Thomas Ringgold, shall refuse to set him out 300 acres of land, at the northernmost bounds of 600 acres of land given by my father, Thomas Ringgold, deceased, unto my said son Thomas, before his death. And whereas my son, James Ringgold, is now the heir apparent unto Captain Robert Vaughan, late of Kent County, deceased—being the eldest son of the now only daughter, and heir of him, the said Vaughan—my will and intent is, that in

liam also left two children, who both died without issue. But the privy councillor was represented by James,[1] the son of Major Ringgold, and who died upon Kent Island, about 1705, leaving three children.[2]

case he, the said James, comes to enjoy the same, that then my aforesaid plantation mentioned in this fourth Article, as also the 300 mentioned in the same Article, be and remain wholly to my son, Thomas Ringgold, and his heirs, for ever." Thomas, it would seem, was the son by a previous marriage. William, John, and Charles, appear to be full brothers of James.

[1] The will of James Ringgold, of Kent Island, then a part of Talbot County, is dated in 1704. See Lib. T. B. No. 2, p. 660. He names his three children, Moses, Mary, and James.

[2] Thomas, the emigrant, and the ancestor of the Ringgolds of Kent Island, of Huntingfield, of Chestertown, and of Fountain-Rock, resided upon the Island, was a cotemporary of Captain Vaughan, and sustained a responsible position upon the bench of the County Court. His son, Major James Ringgold, about 1680, founded New Yarmouth, which stood upon Gray's Inn Creek, and where the courts of the county were once held. For a period of more than two hundred years, the Ringgolds have been one of the leading families of Maryland. They are distinguished in the history of our colonization, and of the early provincial commerce upon the Chester. At the period of the American Revolution, they were conspicuous for their patriotism. They have been represented in the Hall of Congress; and upon the field of battle.

CHAPTER XXII.

The Honorable Robert Clarke.

THE Honorable Robert Clarke arrived within four years[1] of the settlement at St. Mary's; and, in the shipment of goods for the Indian trade, he represented a Roman Catholic missionary, as early as 1639.[2] The same year, he sat as a freeman in the legislature;[3] the following, was a deputy surveyor;[4] and in 1649, the surveyor-general of the province.[5] He was not included in the commission of 1648 for the privy council. But there is

[1] One of the records states he came in 1637; another, in 1638. See Land Office Records, Lib. No. 1, p. 71; and Lib. No. 2, p. 425.

[2] The Reverend Thomas Copley. Land Office Records, Lib. No. 2, p. 38.

[3] An individual, not a delegate. Into some of our early assemblies, the representative system was but partially introduced. Bozman, vol. 2, p. 103.

[4] Lib. No. 1, p. 72.

[5] The commission (see Bozman, Vol. 2, p. 339) is dated in 1648; but he did not immediately enter the office.

evidence of the fact, that he sat in that House of the Assembly, in 1649, and in several subsequent years.[1] Many of the certificates signed by this surveyor-general, are still preserved; and in 1651, he occupied the post of steward (with power to hold the court-baron) of Calverton—a manor of nearly ten thousand acres,[2] at the head of the Wicomico, intended (such was the paternal policy of the feudal proprietary) for a secure "habitation" of "six nations" of Indians, who had desired "to put themselves" under the government's "protection." He also, during the ascendency of the Puritans, openly, in court, confessed his faith in

[1] The documents, in a preceding part of this volume, prove he was a member of the council in 1649. On the 20th of April (O. S.) 1650, he was, for a reason not stated upon the Journal, excused from sitting. See Lib. No. 3, p. 55. In 1654, also, he was a privy councillor. See Lib. No. 1, p. 521. In 1648 he was a burgess (see Lib. No. 2, pp. 293, 294) and held nine proxies. In 1658 he was a judge of the Provincial Court. Lib. "S. 1658 to 1662, Judgments," p. 15. In 1660 he was again in the council; but did not sympathize with governor Fendall, in his treachery toward the proprietary.

[2] The "six nations" who had desired to be under the proprietary's protection, and for whom, as copyhold tenants, this manor was intended, bore the names of Mattapanians, Wicomocons, Patuxents, Lamasconsons, Highahwixons, and Chopticons. See Bozman, vol. 2, p. 675.

the Roman Catholic Church.[1] Upon a previous surrender, at the battle near the Severn, he was taken prisoner by the Puritans;[2] and then treated as a rebel. Tried by a "council of war," but saved "by the petitions of the women,"[3] he was next fined ten thousand pounds of tobacco.[4] Unable to pay the mulct, he assigned various bills to the amount of three thousand; and surrendered his plantation upon Britton's Bay.[5] About six months later, in a state of "deep distress," without the means of "subsistence" either for his "children" or for "himself," he submitted a petition. And the court, composed of Capt. Fuller and other leading Puritans, gave him a temporary possession of the land.[6] In 1657, his bond was

[1] "Robert Clarke, Gent., hath openly in court confessed himself to be a Roman Catholic; owning the Pope's supremacy." See Proceedings of the Provincial Court, October Term, 1655; Land Office Records, Lib. No. 3, p. 156. This was many months after the battle near the Severn.

[2] Bozman, vol. 2, p. 527; and Records of the Land Office, Lib. No. 3, p. 163.

[3] Bozman, vol. 2, p. 688.

[4] Land Office Records, Lib. No. 3, pp. 156 and 157.

[5] Same Liber, pp. 156, 157.

[6] The following is the order passed by the court in 1656:— "Whereas Robert Clarke, Gent., hath petitioned to this court for

required.[1] He never succeeded in reclaiming his fortunes; and, in his will, dated in 1664, there appears but little property.[2] His posterity was dispersed through various parts of the province; and, in 1686, died his eldest son, John, a resident of St. Mary's County, holding land upon a branch of St. Thomas's Creek,[3] in Charles County; and leaving John, Robert, Benjamin, and two other children.[4] The only marriage of the privy councillor

some relief in his exceeding deep distress, not having any way of subsistence for himself and children; the court taking it into consideration, have thought fit and ordered that the plantation of the said Clarke, formerly made over unto the public for part of satisfaction of a fine imposed upon the said Clarke for his late rising up in arms and other great crimes at that time committed, be delivered into the hands of him the said Clarke for his present relief, without which he is likely to perish. And further, if the said Clarke should sell the said plantation, that then he is to pay the one half of what it shall be sold for, in part of the said fine, when it shall be demanded." Lib. No. 3, pp. 178, 179.

[1] Land Office Records, Lib. No. 3, p. 317; and p. 349.

[2] He names his children, John, Robert, Thomas, and Mary. Gives the most of his estate to John; and half the value of a horse "to the Church." See his will, Testamentary Records at Annapolis, Lib. No. 1, 1635 to 1674, pp. 217–218.

[3] Rent-roll for St. Mary's and Charles, vol. 2, fol. 314; and Land Office Records, Lib. No. 6, p. 223.

[4] See will of John, Lib. G. p. 193. The name of Clarke occurs

mentioned upon the records, was the one to Jane, the widow[1] of Nicholas Causin, the ancestor of the family which held the "Manor of Causin," now represented by the Honorable John M. S. Causin.

so frequently that it is very difficult to trace the descendants of the privy councillor. But the reader who may be interested in this subject, is referred to the following sources of information, in the Register's Office at Annapolis:—Wills of Thomas, in 1675, Lib. No. 2, p. 247; John, Lib. H., p. 48; John, Lib. H. p. 177; Robert, Lib. T. B., p. 375; John, Lib. J. C.—W. B., No. 2, Part 2, p. 32; Thomas, Lib. W. B., No. 5, p. 375; Edward, Lib. W. B., No. 6, p. 8; William, Lib. T. B., No. 1, p. 51; Thomas, same Liber, p. 280; and Robert, Lib. W. B., No. 1, p. 438. There is also the will, in 1689 (see Lib. T. B., No. 2, p. 727) of Robt. Clarke, "of the parish of St. Giles, Without Cripple-Gate, London," but who had lived in Maryland, "in the West Indies" (as America was then called); and who was probably one of the Hon. Robt. Clarke's descendants. John's, in Lib. H., on p. 48, is dated the 7th of May, 1680, "according to the computation of the Holy Catholic Church."

[1] Land Office, Lib. No. 7, p. 132.

CHAPTER XXIII.

The Honorable Thomas Hatton.

THE Honorable Thomas Hatton, it would seem, was the son of John Hatton; and, there is hardly a doubt, lived at London,[1] before his arrival. It is said, his family (which came in 1648[2]) had sprung from that of Sir Christopher Hatton, the lord

[1] John Hatton—a brother, I presume, of the secretary—in his will of 1654 (see Records at Annapolis, Lib. No. 1, 1635 to 1674, p. 519) speaks of his "late father, John Hatton;" of his brothers Thomas, Samuel, and Henry; and his sisters Sarah and Susan. The lands left him by his father, he gives his brother Thomas; and appoints him one of his executors. Most of the family, it seems, lived in England; and the testator, although then on a visit to Maryland, resided at London. The godfather of the secretary's son, Thomas, was "one of the clerks in the Six-Clerks' Office, Chancery Lane," in the same city. See the silver spoon given, about 1650, by the godfather, Thomas Motham, on p. 186, Lib. No. 1, Records of the Land Office.

[2] The secretary himself states, that he came, with his wife, his two sons (Robert and Thomas), and his three white servants, in 1648; and that the following year arrived, under his auspices, the widow, and William, Richard, Elinor, and the other children of his

chancellor in the reign of Elizabeth, and so much admired by the queen for his graceful person and his elegant style of dancing. And the tradition, to some extent, is confirmed, not only by the existence in both families of the same baptismal names,[1] but also by that sense of beauty,[2] which was a characteristic not less of the honorable

deceased brother Richard. Land Office Records, Lib. No. 2, p. 613.

[1] "Sir Robert Hatton was a brother," says Burke, "of Sir Thomas Hatton, baronet; and of Sir Christopher Hatton, K.B., father of Lord Hatton, and ancestor of George Finch Hatton, Earl of Winchilsea." Burke's Dictionary of the Landed Gentry, Vol. 2, p. 1287. The names also of Richard, Henry, John, William, and Sarah, occur both in Burke and upon our early records. Thomas, indeed, is found frequently in the history of the English, as well as of the provincial family.

[2] The following note from the secretary, introducing Mr. John De Courcy (then written Coursey), is a fine specimen of the author's style—a model both of terseness and of elegance. John De Courcy was a brother of the Honorable Henry De Courcy; and subsequently the clerk of Kent County:

"Mr. Bradnox,—. . . . The bearer hereof, Mr. John Coursey, upon the invitation of some friends, comes amongst you to try his fortunes at Kent. His quality and good carriage will, I know, purchase respect from all; and especially from yourself and Mistress Bradnox, whose courtesy and respect to strangers, especially to those of the better sort, hath never been wanting. And, therefore, I shall not need to use many words of commendation in his behalf.

secretary of Maryland than of the distinguished statesman of England. The armorial bearings of the Hattons of London were :—"*Argent, three hurts, each charged with a bend of the first; on a chief vert, an eagle displayed or.*" And their crest was :—"*A demi-bear rampant sable.*"[1]

Besides the offices of secretary and of privy councillor (the commissions for which were dated on the same day,[2] in the year 1648), he held the post of attorney-general of the province.[3] Like the other councillors appointed in 1648, he went into office, it would seem, at the commencement of the Assembly, in 1649. It is supposed he brought from England the draft of "The Act concerning Religion." The official power and rank conferred

But desiring, with my wife, to be kindly remembered to yourself, and Mistress Bradnox; Rest;

"Your assured, loving friend, Thomas Hatton,

"St. Mary's, Feb. 1653.

"The superscription—To his much respected friend Mr. Thos. Bradnox, at the Isle of Kent, in Maryland." See Court Record, at Chester-town, commencing in 1647.

[1] Burke's General Armory.

[2] Bozman, vol. 2, p. 649, and p. 651.

[3] In 1652, and I presume other years, he was the attorney-general. Land Office Records, Lib. No. 1, p. 302.

upon our early secretaries were very great.[1] The present secretaryship of State is but the shadow of the original office, under the dominion of the first lord proprietary. Although there is no evidence of the contingency, upon which he was authorized to act, we know he also received a commission appointing him to the post of governor.[2] In 1652, about the beginning of the revolutionary measures under the commissioners from the English commonwealth, he was removed from the secretaryship;[3] re-instated in July, the same year;[4] and again deprived of the office, in the month of August, 1654.[5] Before the Puritan Assembly at Patuxent, the last-named year, he appeared with Mr. Chandler, the other burgess from St. Mary's; and, in view of his "oath" to Lord Baltimore, as well as

[1] The secretary sat, not only in the privy council, but also upon the bench of the High Provincial Court. And great weight was attached to his opinions. The office also of chancellor was usually annexed to the secretaryship.

[2] The latter part of 1649, Gov. Stone having occasion to be absent from the province, appointed Thomas Green governor; in case of his refusal, Mr. Hatton. Bozman, vol. 2, p. 377. In 1650, also, I perceive, he was appointed. Lib. No. 2, p. 615.

[3] Bozman, vol. 2, p. 681.

[4] Bozman, vol. 2, p. 682.

[5] Bozman, vol. 2, p. 685.

other reasons then reduced to writing, but now unfortunately lost, he refused to sit in that body.[1] At the battle of 1655, in the service of the proprietary, he lost his life. An order was issued for the "subsistence" of his widow out of his lordship's "rents;" and every disposition manifested, in testimony of respect for his memory, and of gratitude for his noble fidelity.[2] Remarkable not more for moderation than for decision; discharging his duty in every private and official relation; a Protestant,[3] but not a bigot; the ornament of his own faith, but distinguished for his loyalty to the charter, and to the person of the Roman Catholic proprietary;

[1] Bozman, vol. 2, p. 508.

[2] Bozman, vol. 2, p. 698.

[3] He was one of the signers of the Protestant Declaration. The case of Gardiner (Bozman, vol. 2, p. 493) proves also how ready was the secretary to resist every attempt to seduce his ward and niece, Eleanor Hatton, from the faith of her family. And his nephew, William, married Elizabeth, the daughter (See Rev. William Wilkinson's will, Lib. No. 1, 1635 to 1674, p. 190) of the first Protestant clergyman (an Anglo-Catholic) who arrived in St. Mary's after the landing of the Maryland Pilgrims. See arrival (Land Office Records, Lib. No. 3, p. 62) of "William Wilkinson, clerk," in 1650, with his wife Mary, his daughters Rebecca and Elizabeth, and several other persons including his indented servants. The secretary's wife was also the godmother of Mathew, the son of William Stone, the Protestant governor. See p. 65.

he presents to the student one of the most interesting characters in the history of the colonization of Maryland. A son and grandson, both bearing his own baptismal name, died, it would seem, in Maryland; the one, in 1676,[1] the other in 1701;[2] the former (or a cousin also called Thomas), having lived some time at Tewkesbury, in Gloucestershire, England;[3] the latter, disposing, by his will, of the right to a large tract, not then fully confirmed, but due to him, as heir to the "Secretary of Maryland;" and granted, probably, in token of the grateful recollections cherished by the proprietary, for the noble sacrifice at the battle of 1655. I

[1] Will of Thomas Hatton of St. Mary's County, "gentleman," in Lib. No. 2, 1674 to 1704, on p. 381. Names his only son Thomas; his sisters, Margaret and Rebecca "Wahop;" and several of the Hansons, who seem to be his relations.

[2] Will of Thomas Hatton, of St. Mary's County, also styled "gentleman," in Lib. T. B., p. 120. He possibly had a posthumous son; but the only child named in the will is Elizabeth, to whom he gives "Hunting-Creek," surveyed (see Rent Roll for St. Mary's County, No. 1, Manors, fol. 2) for the secretary, in 1655.

[3] Thomas (the son, I presume of the Hon. Thomas Hatton) lived at Tewkesbury, about 1674; and gave Samuel of Maryland a power of attorney relating to the claim arising upon the death of his brother John. Lib. M. M., 1672 to 1675, Judgments, p. 193, and pp 578–580.

doubt if there is now living a lineal descendant of the same surname anywhere in America. But the Hattons of Piscataway are related to the family, through William, the nephew of the secretary, and the son-in-law of the Rev. William Wilkinson. William Hatton died at an advanced age in 1712, naming his children, Joseph Hatton and Penelope Middleton; and giving to each of his grand-children (including Hatton Middleton), "a gold ring," as the "token" of his "love." He also divided between his children, the home plantation, consisting of "Thompson's Rest," and "Rich Hill."[1]

[1] Will of William, Lib. W. B., No. 5, p. 432. In tracing the descent of the Hattons, near Piscataway, I am indebted, for the use of several land-papers, to the kindness of the Hon. William H. Tuck, of the Court of Appeals.

CHAPTER XXIV.

Mr. Cuthbert Fenwick.

We now descend from the Upper to the Lower House—from the privy councillors to the burgesses—from the representatives of the proprietary to the delegates of the planters, and of the other freemen of the province. The leading member of this body, one who breathed the spirit of Copley, of Cornwallis, and of Calvert, it would seem, was Mr. Cuthbert Fenwick; a sincere believer in the faith of the old Latin church; one of the original Pilgrims of 1634; and the fairest exponent of that system of religious liberty, which had constituted the very corner-stone of the first settlement under the charter. Many, also, are his descendants in the United States. They have held a distinguished rank in the field of civil and of military services. And they have been ornaments, not only of the priesthood, but also of the hierarchy of the American Roman Catholic church. Some still linger among us; our neighbors, and our friends. Through evil, and through good, after the lapse of many years, in the midst of vast social and political revolutions, they have clung, with the fondness of children, to the faith of their first forefather. Is there no gratitude among Protestants? Will the Protestant flinch from the performance of a plain historical duty? Shall he, who inherits a pure Protestant blood, an unbroken Protestant faith, through eight generations, from the age of Elizabeth; whose first Protestant ancestor of the provincial line reached the shores of the Chesapeake but a year after the passage of the memorable Toleration Act, hesitate for one moment in doing justice to the memory of the early Roman Catholic law-givers of Maryland?

Fenwick was the seat of a distinguished family of the same name, in the county of Northumberland, England.[1] And *Fenwick* was the manor erected for the early colonist, in what was subsequently Resurrection hundred, St. Mary's County.[2]

[1] Burke's General Armory; Art. Fenwick, at Fenwick, in Northumberland.

[2] Fenwick Manor was surveyed for Cuthbert Fenwick, in 1651.

In Maryland, also, I am told, there was an old signet ring containing the arms of the Fenwicks, of Fenwick manor; and, it is said, that Cuthbert was a descendant of the Fenwicks in Northumberland County. But history has a more solid foundation than mere oral tradition; and nothing, I regret, can positively be asserted respecting the armorial bearings of the Fenwicks, of St. Mary's; or even their English original, beyond the relationship to the Eltonheads.

Of Captain Cornwallis, the chief councillor of the governor in 1634, and one of the noblest spirits in the band of original Pilgrims, Mr. Fenwick was the special *protégé*.[1] For many years, also, from his arrival, did he hold a great variety of confidential trusts and responsible agencies; living at "The Cross,"[2] during the captain's frequent voyages to England; and transacting, with strict fidelity, all his important business upon the manor.

It is upon the Patuxent. Rent Roll for St. Mary's & Charles, vol. 1, fol. 55.

[1] Land Office Records, Lib. A. B. & H., p. 244.

[2] The name of Capt. Cornwallis's manor-house. The manor, itself, was called "Cornwallis's Cross." Rent Roll for St. Mary's County; also Lib. No. 1, pp. 115–117, and elsewhere.

So intimate was the relationship, that he was summoned on one occasion (the only case of so peculiar a kind of representation, I believe, upon the records), by a special writ, to sit as the "*attorney*" of the councillor, at a meeting of the General Assembly.[1] More, also, on account of the enmity towards Cornwallis than any ground of personal dislike, was he plundered by Captain Ingle,[2] the pirate, the man who gloried in the name of "The Reformation."[3] In the grant of land for the early Roman Catholic missions, his name and services, it appears, were used. It seems, also, he was inti-

[1] This was in 1640. Bozman, vol. 2, p. 171.

[2] He was, about 1645, surprised by Ingle's party, and treacherously confined as a prisoner, on board that pirate's ship; the manor-house of Capt. Thomas Cornwallis much injured, and also plundered of its servants, valuable furniture, and other property. On his way to Accomac, Va., he was also robbed of his "clothes," and "papers." Lib. No. 1, pp. 432–433; pp. 572–573; pp. 582–583; and p. 584. Lib. No. 2, p. 354; and pp. 616–617.

[3] The world, alas! is governed more by the shadow than by the substance! Here is a man from Wapping, in Middlesex, England (see Lib. No. 1, pp. 377)—a sea-captain of a reckless sort of courage—plundering a missionary, and many other Roman Catholics of the province; and, by universal consent, a pirate; yet giving to his very ship the name of "The Reformation!" Lib. No. 1, p. 224. Triumphant, for a short time, in his rebellion; he did a great deal of injury to the proprietary.

mate with the Rev. Thomas Copley; and often in contact with Governor Leonard Calvert; took part in the little engagement of 1635, upon a tributary of the Chesapeake, between the pinnace commanded by Warren (the lieutenant of Clayborne), and the two armed boats under the command of Cornwallis;[1] and sat in the Assembly of 1638, the earliest of which we have a satisfactory account.[2] As an individual freeman, he had a seat also in the legislature of the subsequent year.[3] And few, if any, of the original colonists were members more frequently of the legislative body. Again: we find him aiding the government in the regulation of the Indian trade with the colonists;[4] and about the same time, he reported the information he had obtained respecting the murder of Rowland Williams, of Accomac[5]—a case which engaged the

[1] Bozman, vol. 2, p. 35; and p. 65, where the name is written "Hemirk," but doubtless intended for "Fenwick." The lieutenant and two of his men were killed; and one was lost on the captain's side. Cornwallis's boats were called "The St. Helen," and "The St. Margaret." Clayborne's next officer in command was subsequently convicted at St. Mary's.

[2] Bozman, vol. 2, p. 65.

[3] Bozman, vol. 2, p. 103.

[4] Bozman, vol. 2, p. 115.

[5] The Report is dated May 8, 1638." See Lib. No. 2, pp. 83–84.

prompt attention of the governor, and resulted in the union of Maryland with her sister colony,[1] in the punishment of the *Nanticokes*. In 1644, he held a commissionership in St. Mary's[2]—an office out of which grew that of the early county court judge. He was the foreman of many of the most important trial juries,[3] at the provincial court; the first member of the financial committee,[4] and probably the speaker, in the Lower House of the Roman Catholic Assembly of 1649;[5] and, in the Protestant one of 1650, the chairman of a joint committee[6] upon the "Laws," including Governor Green and Colonel Price from the Upper House. The latter part of his life, he resided upon Fenwick manor; and died about the year 1655.[7] Nothing

[1] Lib. No. 1, p. 159.

[2] Bozman, vol. 2, p. 280.

[3] In the case, for instance, of the Piscataway Indians already quoted.

[4] Lib. No. 2, p. 489.

[5] From the report of the financial committee, the only remaining fragment of the Journal, it is evident that he performed some special or honorable service, besides that of an ordinary member.

[6] Lib. No. 3, p. 56.

[7] His Will is dated "March 6, 1654." Lib. S., 1658 to 1662, "Judgments," Court of Appeals (in the Armory), p. 219.

occurs upon the record, to lessen, in the least, the esteem to which he is so justly entitled as a legislator, and a public officer; a Christian, and a man.

Mr. Fenwick bore the name of one of the most celebrated saints,[1] in the history of the early English Church; held a tract bounded by St. Cuthbert's Creek;[2] although present, did not sign the

[1] In speaking of the ravages of the Danes, during the ninth century, Sir Francis Palgrave says: "The Pagans, under Halfdane, destroyed all the churches and monasteries. The ruin of the Cathedral of Lindisfairne, in particular, was lamented as the greatest misfortune of the age. Cuthbert, one of the prelates of this see, canonized by the grateful veneration of the English, was considered as the patron saint of the North; and the island of Lindisfairne was viewed as holy land."

In a note, he adds:—"The body of St. Cuthbert was saved when the church of Lindisfairne was destroyed, and after many migrations it was deposited in the Cathedral of Durham, to which city the see of Lindisfairne was transferred (A. D. 990); the present bishops of Durham being the successors of the bishops of Lindisfairne. The corpse of St. Cuthbert was deposited in a magnificent shrine, which was destroyed at the time of the Reformation." "In 1827, a skeleton, supposed to be that of St. Cuthbert, was disinterred by the Rev. James Raine. The body had been deposited with some most curious relics of the Anglo-Saxon age—amongst them, the cross." Palgrave's History of the Anglo-Saxons, p. 124. The engraving of St. Cuthbert's cross is on p. 142 of the History.

[2] Rent Roll for St. Mary's and Charles, vol. 1, fol. 55.

Protestant Declaration; upon the questions arising between the two religious parties, in the Protestant Assembly of 1650, voted with the Roman Catholic members;[1] gave a legacy to each of the Roman Catholic priests, in testimony of his faith in the Church of Rome;[2] to say nothing of the further evidence derived from the fact, that so many of his descendants are still members of the same communion.

In 1649, then a widower, and the father of Thomas (who seems to have died young), of Cuthbert, Ignatius, and "Teresa;"[3] Mr. Fenwick married Jane,[4] the widow of Robert Moryson (the name is written upon the record, indistinctly), of

[1] See, in various places, the proceedings of the Assembly, in 1650, Lib. No. 3, Land Office; also the signatures, in the same Liber, on p. 57, to the letter of this Assembly, intended for Lord Baltimore.

[2] By some of the early Roman Catholics (for example, by Robert Clarke) legacies were given "to the church"—meaning, of course, the Roman Catholic; by others, to the well known priests, Lawrence Starkie and Francis Fitzherbert, always, either tacitly or avowedly, in token of their faith in the same church; and by a third class (Cuthbert Fenwick, for instance), simply "unto Mr. Starkie," and "unto Mr. Fitzherbert." See Mr. Fenwick's Will, Lib. S. 1658 to 1662, Judgments, p. 219.

[3] Land Office Records, Lib. No. 2, p. 515.

[4] Lib. S. 1658 to 1662, Judgments, p. 218.

"Kecoughtan" County, Va.; the sister also of William Eltonhead[1] (the privy councillor of Md.), and Richard Eltonhead[2] (of "Eltonhead," Lancaster County, England); and the niece of Edward[3] Eltonhead, one of the "masters[4]" of the English "High Court of Chancery." He had issue, also, by his last marriage; and his widow died in 1660.[5] The

[1] Lib. No. 3, p. 262; Lib. S. 1658 to 1662, Judgments, p. 135; and pp. 219–220. Also Testamentary Records, Lib. No. I., p. 94.

[2] Lib. F. F. 1665 to 1669, Judgments (Court of Appeals), in the Armory, p. 788.

[3] Land Office, Lib. A. B. and H., p. 165.

[4] Lib. 5, 1658 to 1662, Judgments (Court of Appeals), p. 1; and Lib. No. 3 (Land Office), p. 413.

[5] The social and domestic life of the past constitutes the most interesting branch of history. Mrs. Fenwick's will (see Testamentary Records, Lib. No. 1, p. 114) sheds much light upon the subject; enables us to form some idea of the degree of comfort in the family of this early colonial legislator; and gives a very good key to a bed-chamber, a lady's wardrobe, head-dress, and other articles, in 1660. She bequeaths to her step-daughter, "Teresa," a little bed, a mohair rug, a blanket, a pair of sheets, and "the yellow curtains;" her taffeta suit, and serge coat; all her "fine linen," consisting of aprons, handkerchiefs, head-clothes, &c.; her "wedding-ring;" her hoods, scarfs (except her "great" one), and gloves (except three pair of cotton); and her three petticoats, one of which is a "tufted-holland," another a "new serge," and the third a "spangled" one. She gives to her own three children, Robert, Richard, and John, her "great scarf," all her jewels, "plate," and rings (except the "wedding" one); and to each of them a bed, and pair of cotton gloves. To her stepsons, Cuthbert

children were Robert, Richard, and John.[1] But

and Ignatius, she wills an "ell of taffeta;" to her negro-servant, Dorothy, her "red cotton coat" and some "old linen;" to Esther, her "new maid-servant," all the linen of "the coarser sort;" to Thomas, the Indian, two pair of shoes, a matchcoat, and some other things; to Anthumpt, another Indian, several articles of clothing; to Thomas's mother (the "old Indian woman") three yards of cotton; to the Rev. Francis Fitzherbert, a hogshead of tobacco, for five years; to William (a negro) the right to his freedom, provided he pay a hogshead every year to the church, and continue a member; and to the church the same negro, as a slave "for ever," if he leave her communion—one of the few cases of individual intolerance, on the same side, in our early history, and outweighed by a great number of instances, on the other if not, indeed, excusable by the fact, that some of her dearest friends had fallen by the bloody hand of the Puritans, including her own brother, the Hon. Wm. Eltonhead. Take also the following (from Lib. No. 1, Land Office Records, p. 401) about two years before her brother's execution. According to the testimony of Mary Jones, it appears, Martin Kirk and his wife, with Lizy Potter, "had found a way to pay Eltonhead, without weight or scales!" "Hang them!" they added, "Papists! dogs! They shall have no right here; for the governor cannot abide them, but from the teeth outwards." The Vandal outruns the bigot in the case of a noted Protestant of Kent Island, who, entering Capt. Brent's house, and going into the "loft," threw down the captain's books, with the words, "Burn Papists! devils!" This was about the time of Ingle's rebellion. I deem it fair to add, the part of Roger Baxter's testimony relating to the books, was not reduced to writing. But Francis Brooke, a judge of the county court, was present at the taking of the deposition; and states the fact, in his own deposition. Lib. No. 2, p. 387.

[1] See wills of Mr. Fenwick, and his widow Jane. I infer, then,

Cuthbert, his eldest son by a previous marriage, held, under the will, the lordship of Fenwick Manor. The Fenwicks of Cole's Creek, of Cherry-fields, of Pomonkey, and elsewhere, in Maryland; of Kentucky; and (it is said) of the South also (including a well-known officer in the war of 1812); are but some of the off-shoots[1] from the family of Cuthbert, the pilgrim of 1634, and the original lord of the manor. One of the descendants of the early law-giver was a member of the convention, which framed the Constitution of the State, in

that his three youngest sons were, on their mother's side, descendants of the Eltonheads, of Eltonhead; whose arms, according to Burke's General Armory, are—*Quarterly, per fesse indented, sable and argent, on the first quarter three plates.*

[1] The family is so large as to render it impossible to present even a condensed history in any but a work expressly devoted to the department of genealogy. The following wills contain a large body of facts:—Wills of Richard, in 1714, Lib. W. B., No. 5, p. 699; of John, 1720, T. B. No. 1, p. 339; Dorothy, 1724, W. B., No. 1, p. 285; Cuthbert, about 1728, C. C., No. 2, p. 888; Ellen, 1737, T. D., p. 825; Philip, 1750, D. D., No. 6, p. 183; Enock, 1758, B. T., No. 2, p. 582; Joseph, 1758, B. T., No. 2, p. 624; Cuthbert, 1762, D. D., No. 1, in 2 parts, p. 891; Benedict, 1769, W. D., No. 2, p. 251; Bennett, 1770, W. D., No. 3, p. 458; George, 1769, W. D., No. 3, p. 703; Elizabeth, 1771, W. D., No. 4, p. 347; Robert, 1774, W. F., No. 1, p. 113; and Ignatius, 1776, W. F., No. 2. p. 219.

1774–1776;[1] two held a seat in the Senate of Maryland;[2] and a fourth was the consul of the United States, at Bordeaux. Many of them were priests;[3] one was the president of a college;[4] and two were bishops.[5] They are also connected with the Spaldings of St. Mary's, the relations of the bishop of Louisville.[6] And a living descendant of the pilgrim held the post of attorney-general[7]—

[1] Ignatius, of Mary's County.

[2] Athanasius and James; the former closely related to the Cherry-field branch, near St. Inigo's, St. Mary's County; the latter (Col. James), the brother of the bishop of Cincinnati, and the ancestor of the Fenwicks, of Pomonkey, in Charles.

[3] John, the uncle of the bishop of Cincinnati; Enoch, who died in 1827; George, late professor of Rhetoric, in the Novitiate of the Society of Jesus, at Frederick, but now living at Inigo's; the children of Mrs. Young, the sister of Col. Jas. Fenwick; and probably several others; have represented the family in the priesthood. John died about 1814.

[4] Enock, already named, was the president of Georgetown College.

[5] Edward, the first bishop of Cincinnati, and a very near relation to the Fenwicks of Pomonkey; and Benedict, the second bishop of Boston, and the brother of President Fenwick, and Professor Fenwick. Edward died in 1832; Benedict in 1845.

[6] The Rt. Rev. Martin J. Spalding, the present bishop of the diocese. See Elizabeth's will, 1771, W. D. No. 4, p. 347, for the connection with the Spaldings.

[7] Robert James Brent, a Fenwick on the maternal side, and the immediate descendant of the Fenwicks of Pomonkey.

the last link[1] in a long chain of distinguished lawyers from the provincial era of the Hattons, the Lowes, and the Darnalls, down to the days of a Martin, a Taney, and a Richardson.

[1] The office was abolished by the late Constitutional Convention of Maryland.

CHAPTER XXV.

Mr. Philip Conner.

THE time of Mr. Philip Conner's[1] arrival cannot be ascertained; but he came about the year 1645. Under the commandership of Captain Robert Vaughan, in 1647, he was a commissioner of the Isle of Kent;[2] sat, the following year, in the Assembly, as an individual freeman;[3] and was the member from Kent, in 1649.[4] Authorized to issue writs, upon the removal of the captain, in the month of November, 1648;[5] and the only one of the commissioners retained in office, the succeeding

[1] Sometimes spelled "Conyer." Kent Island Records at Chestertown.

[2] Bozman, vol. 2, p. 304.

[3] Capt. Vaughan, in 1648, held 24 voices; Mr. Conner, and Capt. Thomas Bradnox sat, simply, as freemen, without any proxies. Lib. No. 2, pp. 293–294.

[4] Lib. No. 2, pp. 488–489.

[5] Bozman, vol. 2, p. 343.

month, by a Roman Catholic governor;[1] he fortunately, about four years later, escaped the censure of the Puritan commissioners.[2] Free from entanglements of every sort—giving great satisfaction, for a period of many years, by his manner of administering justice—he was elevated, near the close of his life, to the honorable post of commander of the county.[3] His career, in every particular, was marked with discretion; and we might suppose he was a Roman Catholic, living in a Protestant county. But, while no satisfactory clew can be found in his own words or deeds; from the pen of a contemporary, we have the proof, that he was a Protestant.[4]

The will of this early colonist is lost. But from his inventory, it appears, he died about 1660. Judging from the same paper, he lived in a style

[1] Upon Captain Vaughan's re-instatement. Bozman, vol. 2, p. 344.

[2] Vaughan, in 1652, was removed by the Puritan commissioners. See the names of the commissioners sent, in Bozman, vol. 2, p. 454. But Bozman's inference is false. They did visit the island. See Kent Island Records, at Chestertown.

[3] See oldest Land Records, at Chestertown.

[4] The evidence, which is obtained from the will of Thomas Allen, will be given, in a note to the sketch of Capt. Banks's life.

superior to the ordinary level of comfort, at that period.[1] He held "Conner's Neck," "The Wood-yard Thicket," and other tracts, upon Kent Island;[2] and there, lived his descendants also, for several generations. It seems, there was a branch of the family in Dorchester and Somerset; and he has probably a descendant living at Chestertown. His son, Philip,[3] died, about 1700, upon the Isle of Kent,[4] then a part of Talbot; and his grandson, of the same name, in 1722, leaving two brothers and three sons.[5]

[1] The inventory is found in a Record of Wills, and Proceedings in Testamentary cases, beginning in 1657. He had 120 head of cattle, and 34 hogs; 7 feather beds, and 6 rugs; 2 pair of curtains, with valance; 2 flock beds, with 2 rugs; 3 diaper tablecloths; 18 napkins; 8 chairs; 12 wine glasses; and a great variety of other articles.

[2] Lib. No. 12, pp. 572-573. See also Rent Roll for Queen Anne's; for a copy of which, I was indebted, through the kind agency of Judge Chambers, to the late Hon. William Carmichael.

[3] Lib. No. 12, p. 572.

[4] Will of Philip, 1701 (Lib. T. B. p. 350), who gives his son, Philip, "Conner's Neck;" and to his other children Nathaniel, and Charles, "The Wood-yard Thicket." Disposes also of a tract, supposed to be his, on the Elk River.

[5] Will of Philip (witnessed by Nathaniel and Charles, Lib. A. & D., No. 2, p. 196) gives a tract, when recovered, in Kent, near Morgan's Creek, in equal parts, to his sons James, Nathaniel, and

Charles. Will of Nathaniel, his brother, is found in Lib. C. C., No. 2, p. 150. Nathaniel names his son-in-law, Mathew Brown; his daughter, Letitia Brown; and his granddaughter, Mary Brown. There is also the will of John Conner, a merchant of Chestertown, whose children were James and Isabella. He died about 1750.

CHAPTER XXVI.

Mr. William Bretton.

MR. BRETTON arrived, with his wife, Mary (the daughter of Thomas Nabbs), and one child, within three years from the landing of the Pilgrims.[1] He soon afterwards held a large tract* upon Britton's Bay;[2] and many years, lived in Newtown hundred; was a soldier at St. Inigo's Fort, at a very critical period, in the administration of Governor Calvert;[3] and the register of the Provincial Court, under Governor Green, with the power, during the lieutenant-general's absence, to sign writs, "under the governor's name;"[4] kept some of the most important records of the province, till the

[1] He arrived in 1637. Lib. No. 1, p. 69.

[2] In Newtown hundred, and held of the Manor of Little Britain, and also called "Little Britton" (Rent Roll for St. Mary's and Charles, vol. 1, fol. 24); bounded on the south by the Potomac, on the east by Britton's Bay, on the west by St. Clement's Bay, and partly by St. Nicholas's Creek, on the North. Lib. No. 1, p. 69. He certainly lived in Newtown, in 1649. Lib. No. 2, p. 459.

[3] Lib. No. 2, p. 284.

[4] Lib. No. 2, p. 226; and p. 228.

arrival of Mr. Hatton, in 1649;[1] and was the clerk of the Protestant Assembly in 1650.[2] In the legislature of 1648, he held four voices,[3] three of them certainly[4] from Newtown; probably the fourth also. And, from his familiarity with the records, as well as his general knowledge of business, we cannot but presume he was one of the most influential members of the Roman Catholic Assembly in 1649.[5] He is also worthy of remembrance, in consideration of the fact, that he founded one of the first Roman Catholic chapels of the province[6]—a chapel which was erected and sustained by the pious members of his own church in Newtown,[7] and in St. Clement's hundred; which

[1] Lib. No. 2, p. 448.

[2] Bozman, vol. 2, p. 383.

[3] Lib. No. 2, pp. 293–294.

[4] Lib. No. 2, pp. 287–288.

[5] Lib. No. 2, pp. 488–489.

[6] Lib. S. 1658 to 1662, Judgments, p. 1026.

[7] There is evidence, upon various Records. The deed, itself, recites the "unanimous" agreement. And Col. Jarboe, and William Tattershall (planters upon Britton's Bay, and relations of the R. C. privy councillor, Mr. Pile), gave, each of them, a legacy; the former, in 1671, to the Father of "St. Ignatius's Chapel," for the use of the "poor Catholics;" the latter, about 1670, to the "Reverend father" of the same chapel. See Wills, Lib. No. 2, 1674 to 1704, p. 67; and Lib. No. 1, 1635 to 1674, pp. 391–392. Other cases could be cited.

also bore the name of "the patron saint of Maryland."[1]

A mystery clouds the latter part of his life. About 1651, he married Mrs. Temperance Jay.[2] Misfortune seems soon after to have attended him; and his "son" and "daughter" received "alms," at a moment of deep distress.[3] Nor can his will be found; or his posterity traced. But there is no doubt whatever, he was one of the *Roman Catholic* Assemblymen of 1649. He held a tract bounded by *St. William's* Creek;[4] the most striking part of his cattle-mark (*a fleur-de-lis*)[5] was a favorite device

[1] St. Michael was one of the guardian angels. But St. Ignatius was generally regarded the patron saint. See Father White.

[2] Lib. S., 1658 to 1662, Judgments, p. 336–337; and p. 1026.

[3] "There was given to Mr. Bretton's son and daughter an alms, they being in extremity of want." See Statement of Ralph Croutch, at London, in 1662; Lib. B. B., 1663 to 1665, p. 22. Mr. Croutch was one of the executors of Edward Cotton, a colonist.

[4] Lib. S., 1658 to 1662, p. 1026.

[5] To prevent mistakes and disputes, as well as felonies (for many of our early plantations had but few fences, and the flocks and herds often wandered through thick forests, which have long since disappeared), the law of the province required, in the strictest manner, every colonist to register his cattle-mark. On p. 459, in Lib. No. 2, we find:—"William Bretton, gent., recorded his mark of hogs and cattle, viz.: Over and underkeeled, ye right ear, commonly called a *fleur-de-lis*; cropt ye left ear. Which is

with the members of his church, at that period;[1] his name is not among the signers of the Protestant Declaration;[2] and the very phraseology, in his gift of the church-lot, has the unmistakable marks of his sympathy with the faith of the Roman church, and (independently of other evidence) is sufficient to satisfy a reasonable mind.[3]

the true and only mark of ye said William Bretton." It will be observed, that the *fleur-de-lis* (or heraldic lily) differs from the lily of the garden, in having three leaves instead of five. See Burke.

[1] It was a part of the mark of Doctor Thomas Matthews (Lib. No. 2, p. 511), of Col. William Evans (Lib. S., 1658 to 1662, p. 25), and of Doctor Thomas Gerrard (Lib. S., 1658 to 1662, p. 117). These gentlemen were, all, Roman Catholics. See confession of Mathews, Lib. No. 3, p. 157; will of Evans, Lib. No. 1, 1635 to 1674, p. 331; and the faith of Gerrard, in the case of the Rev. Francis Fitzherbert, in another note. I perceive no instance, at this period, in which the *fleur-de-lis*, as a part of the cattle-mark, was adopted by any Protestant.

[2] He was in the Assembly when the Declaration was drawn up and signed. But he was not one of the signers.

[3] The following is from Lib. S. 1658 to 1662, Judgments, p. 1026:

"April ye 12, 1662. This day came Mr. Wm. Bretton, and desired the ensuing to be recorded: viz.

"AD PERPETUAM REI MEMORIAM.

"Forasmuch as divers good and zealous Roman Catholic inhabitants of Newtown, and St. Clement's Bay, have unanimously agreed, amongst themselves, to erect and build a church or chapel whither they may repair on Sundays, and other holy days appointed and commanded by Holy Church; to serve Almighty God; and hear divine service. And the most convenient place for that purpose, desired and pitched upon, by them all, is on a certain parcel of the land belonging to Wm. Bretton, gentleman. Now know ye, that I, William Bretton, of Little-Bretton, in y[e] county of St. Mary's, in the province of Maryland, gentleman; with the hearty, good-liking of my dearly beloved wife, Temperance Bretton; to the greater honor and glory of Almighty God, the Ever-Immaculate Virgin Mary, and all Saints; have given, and do hereby freely for ever give, to the behoof of the said Roman Catholic inhabitants, and their posterity, or successors, Roman Catholics, so much land, as they shall build y[e] said church or chapel on; which, for their better convenience, they may frequent, to serve Almighty God, and hear divine service, as aforesaid; with such other land adjoining to y[e] said church or chapel, convenient likewise for a churchyard, wherein to bury their dead; containing about one acre and a half of ground, situate and lying on a dividend of land called Bretton's Outlet, and on the east side of y[e] said dividend, near to y[e] head of the creek called St. William's Creek, which falleth into St. Nicholas's Creek, and near unto the narrowest place of y[e] freehold of Little-Bretton, commonly called The Straits," &c., &c.

Could not this interesting little chapel's history yet be written? The deed surely indicates, with sufficient distinctness, the spot where it stood. It is dated the "tenth" of November 1661."

CHAPTER XXVII.

Mr. Richard Browne.

Nothing is known of the ancestry, birth-place, or posterity of Mr. Browne; and less, indeed, of his own immediate life, than that of any member of the Assembly in 1649. A part of the obscurity arises from the fact, that two persons of his name lived here about the same period; the one having arrived about the year 1638;[1] the other, during the month of July, 1648.[2] The former, it seems, took the "oath of fealty," "June 27th, 1647;"[3] and the latter, the "14th of November," 1648.[4] The name of "*Richard Browne*" also appears among the members of the preceding

[1] He was one of the securities, that year, upon the bond of Lieut. Wm. Lewis, the Roman Catholic. See Lewis's case, in Bozman, vol. 2, p. 598.

[2] Lib. No. 2, p. 458.

[3] Council Proceedings, from 1636 to 1657, in the Executive Chamber, p. 144.

[4] Council Proceedings, p. 145.

Assembly;[1] and is affixed, about a year later, to the Protestant Declaration.[2] One of them (the emigrant of 1648) usually had the prefix of "*Mr.*", or the addition of "*gentleman.*" The other, probably, belonged to the class of yeomen.[3] The former lived upon Clement's manor, the latter part of 1649.[4] The residence of the latter, during the same year, it is now impossible to give. We may suppose, the "gentleman" was the member of the Assembly; and also one of the persons of consideration, in the province, who signed the Declaration. But the evidence of the Assemblyman's identity with the Protestant, is, by no means, conclusive. The result of the investigation is anything but satisfactory.

[1] Lib. No. 2, pp. 488, 489.

[2] See Declaration, Bozman, vol. 2, p. 672.

[3] He rarely had either the prefix or the addition.

[4] Lib. No. 3, pp. 96, 97. The plantation upon the manor was bought (see Lib. No. 2, p. 508) "June 29, 1649;" and sold, by "Richard Brown, gentleman" (see Lib. No. 3, pp. 101, 102), "unto George Manners and his assigns," in the year 1651.

CHAPTER XXVIII.

Mr. George Manners.

But little also can be gleaned from the records relating to the life of Mr. Manners. Enough, however, remains to warrant the supposition, he was a soldier in the march under Colonel Price, in 1647, against a hostile band of eastern-shore Indians;[1] and we know he held a seat in the

[1] The *Nanticokes* and the *Wicomicks*. Bozman (vol. 2, p. 310) doubts if the "expedition" ever "took place." That it did, is evident. "Jas. Lindsay, at ye request of Capt. Jno. Price, saith upon his oath, that Lieut. Wm. Lewis was the first man, that drew sword, and entered the house, pulling the mat from off the house; and brought forth out of the house an Indian woman, and a child; delivering her to the guard, at ye march on ye Eastern shore, sometime in July last; and further he saith not. George Manners deposeth the same, and addeth further, that at the entering of the house, Lt. Lewis gave the word 'Give fire.' And an Indian bolting out of ye house, the said Lt. Lewis commanded his party to give fire upon the Indian also. And when both parties came together, Capt. Price commanded the whole party to march, and bid them not to wrong, or take any thing from any Indian, or shoot at any Indian. And so they marched near upon two miles

Assembly of the province, during the years 1649[1] and 1650.[2] We have also the evidence of the fact, that he was a Roman Catholic. Present at the signing of the Declaration, he did not affix his name. Upon the test questions of 1650, he acted with the Roman Catholic members of the Assembly.[3] And he gave a legacy to the church, of which he was a member. He died in 1651,[4] leaving his sons William and Edward, and his daughter Barbara.

back again, not shooting any gun. But the Indians, gathering in great companies about our men, shot a man of ours in the rear. And then Capt. Price commanded the company to give fire; and not before. Walter Gweast deposeth *idem ad verba.*" See Lib. No. 2, pp. 306–307.

[1] Lib. No. 2, pp. 488–489.

[2] Lib. No. 3, p. 47.

[3] See, for the sake of illustration, Bozman, vol. 2, p. 389; and Lib. No. 3 (Land-Office Records), p. 57.

[4] The possessions of our forefathers, besides their lands and servants, consisted chiefly of flocks and herds. "I give and bequeath to the church one red cow-calf." See will of Mr. Manners, Lib. No. 1, 1635 to 1674, p. 32. "Church," without an express declaration to the contrary, always, during that period, signified the Roman Catholic. And the gift was in token of the testator's faith. See (*ex. gra.*) the wills of the well-known Roman Catholics, Robt. Clarke, and Barnaby Jackson. See also, on the other hand, the note to p. 235 of this volume.

CHAPTER XXIX.

Captain Richard Banks.

ASSUMING, that Captain Banks was one of the Protestant members of the Assembly in 1649 ; we are struck with the magnanimity, which subsequently marked his career. Of his ancestry, nothing is positively known ; and it is doubtful if he left any descendants. But we are informed of the fact, that he married Margaret Hatton, the widow of the secretary's brother.[1] He arrived in 1646.[2] His house was robbed by Ingle's accomplices ;[3] and he arrested, about the same time, five Indians,[4] who were suspected of "felony," but soon afterwards tried and acquitted. In the Assembly of 1648, he represented twenty-four freemen ;[5] and we know,

[1] Lib. No. 1, p. 440.

[2] Lib. No. 2, p. 458 ; and Lib. A. B. and H., p. 15.

[3] Robbed of tobacco sold to Capt. Cornwallis. Lib. No. 2, p. 303.

[4] They were *Patuxents*. Lib. No. 2, p. 343.

[5] On the 20th of January (O. S.) he held, from New-town,

he sat in the same body, during the year 1649.[1] In 1652, he held the responsible post of a councillor, under the sway of the Puritans;[2] yet in 1655, he was on the side of Governor Stone. Satisfied of the purity of his intentions, the victorious party, within a few months after the battle, gave him a discharge;[3] but the following October (having "done something" offensive at the election of burgesses), he was required to give security for his "good abearance."[4] From all, that can now be ascertained, we have reason for the belief, that his character was in the highest degree estimable. His pledge for the redemption, from captivity, of an orphan child, is honorable to his memory;[5]

"19 proxies" (Lib. No. 2, pp. 287, 288); and, on the 28th of the same month (p. 293, 294), "24 voices."

[1] Lib. No. 2, pp. 488, 489.

[2] Bozman, vol. 2, p. 681.

[3] "Lieut. Richard Banks and Thomas Tunnell, being found in arms against the present government; and pleading they were misled by the protestation of Capt. Stone, who said, he had power from the Lord Protector; and also did surrender a fort upon the first summons; are discharged from further trouble, in the action, upon their submission, and good forbearance to the present government." Lib. No. 3, p. 138, Proceedings of the Provincial Court, April Term, 1655.

[4] Lib. No. 3 p. 156.

[5] An order was passed by the Assembly for the ransom of Thos.

and illustrates a trait, for which he seems to have been distinguished. His acceptance of an office under the Puritans, suggests the idea that he was a Protestant; but his subsequent sympathy with the government of the proprietary, and the part he took in the contest of 1655, would render the supposition extremely doubtful. A colonist of his surname (probably his son), was unquestionably a member of the English church;[1] and this fact strengthens the opinion, that the Assembly-man of 1649 held the same faith. But the probability is weakened by the further fact, that the name of Banks occurs very frequently upon the records;

Allen's two children; and they were required to serve the persons who might advance the money. But on "the 15th of September, 1650, lieutenant" (subsequently captain) "Banks freely engageth himself to satisfy the 900 pounds of tobacco and cask, for the redemption of Thomas, the son of Thos. Allen, deceased; according to the order of the Assembly for that purpose; without any consideration of servitude, or any other consideration whatever, but his free love, and affection. Witness his hand, ye day and year abovesaid. Richard Banks." See the Assembly's Order (Lib. No. 3, p. 42–43) for the payment to the Indians; and Capt. Banks's Engagement, Lib. No. 3, p. 26.

[1] "Declaring myself hereby to be a Christian, and to hold the Catholic faith, as it is established by the canonical doctrine of the Church of England, into which I was baptized." Will of Thos. Bankes, in 1684, Lib. G., p. 126. *Catholic* is, here, expressly defined

and that many who bore it, were not at all related to each other. Accident, however, sometimes rewards the diligence of the student. From an incidental source, we have the proof, that Captain Banks was a Protestant.[1]

[1] "Now for the disposal of my children," says Thos. Allen, "I would not have them live with any Papist. For my eldest son, Thomas, if he pleases to live with one of the overseers of this my will; he may, during his pleasure." Capt. Banks was one of the overseers. See the Will, Lib. No. 1, 1635 to 1674, p. 15. In the same paper, he suggests to his overseers to offer another son to Mr. Phil. Conner, who had expressed a desire to adopt one of the children. The will is dated in 1648; and written, under great anxiety, from an apprehension of violence, or some other cause. The next thing, we learn, is the captivity of his orphans among the Indians He was an Assembly-man in 1648.

CHAPTER XXX.

Mr. John Maunsell.

MR. MAUNSELL[1] arrived, as early as the year 1637;[2] and lived in St. Clement's hundred in 1642.[3] It would seem, his residence about ten years later, was in the same part of St. Mary's county;[4] and either there, or in the adjacent hundred of Newtown,[5] we cannot but suppose, he may be traced, during the year 1649, when he held a seat in the General Assembly of the province. He did not take up many tracts of land; and all his possessions were indeed rather small; but he is generally styled "planter" upon the records. And, while his name is not often connected with important events in our early history, yet surely

[1] Spelt also "Mansell."

[2] Lib. No. 1, pp. 68–69.

[3] Records of the Executive Chamber, Proceedings of the Assembly, Lib. 1637 to 1658, pp. 209–215.

[4] Lib. B. B., 1663 to 1665, Judgments, pp. 153–154.

[5] Lib. A. B. and H., p. 167.

two incidents demand a notice—the plunder of his house by Ingle's piratical party[1]—and his relationship towards the memorable Assembly of 1649.[2] The evidence of his faith in the Roman Catholic church, is purely circumstantial, but not the less conclusive or satisfactory. The inference is drawn from the absence of everything (so far as his life can now be illustrated), like the least taint of disloyalty toward the proprietary; from the historical traditions connected with the name of "*Maunsell*;"[3] from the faith of the gentleman, under

[1] "John Maunsell maketh oath that about five years since (when Richard Ingle, mariner, and his accomplices, plundered divers of the inhabitants of this province of Maryland) divers persons of his, the said Ingle's party, plundered and took away from this deponent's house, in Maryland aforesaid, one hogshead of tobacco, which then had been paid, and belonged to Mr. Cuthbert Fenwick, or to Capt. Thos. Cornwallis; and that John Rablay, of Virginia, was then in company of them that so plundered and took away the said tobacco; which Rablay was one of them, that was most active and busy in employments of that nature.

"Jurat, 5 die November, 1649, *coram me*,

Lib. No. 2, p. 524. "THOS. HATTON."

[2] Lib. No. 2, pp. 488, 489.

[3] The name of one distinguished, but fifty years later, in the Roman Catholic missions of Maryland. The records are lost, and I cannot trace the relationship; but presume he was a member of the same family. Thomas was his first name.

whose special care, and immediate auspices, he came to Maryland;[1] from the year of his arrival, so distinguished for the large number of Roman Catholic emigrants,[2] and so near the landing of the original Pilgrims at St. Mary's, as to warrant the *presumption* (apart from other reasons), that he was a disciple of the same church; from the hostility manifested (chiefly, indeed, toward Captain Cornwallis, but partly, also, we may suppose, against himself) by the Catholic-hating, Puritan pirate;[3] from the well-known Roman Catholic prefix to a tract surveyed for him;[4] from the absence of his name (a fact of very great weight) from a Declaration signed by so many of the most prominent Protestants, including (it would seem) some of his neighbors;[5] but especially from the

[1] Mr. William Bretton, the Roman-Catholic Assembly-man of 1649. See Lib. No. 1, pp. 68–69.

[2] The Rev. Thos. Copley, Messrs. Wm. Bretton, Luke Gardiner, Thos. Mathews, John Lewger, and the members of Mr. Lewger's family, were some of the Roman Catholics, who came in 1637. See Lib. No. 1, pp. 19–20.

[3] See Mr. Maunsell's preceding deposition.

[4] "St. John's," consisting of 100 acres, on the west side of Britton's Bay, was surveyed for Mr. Maunsell in 1649. Rent-Roll for St. Mary's and Charles, vol. 1, fol. 26.

[5] In Lib. B. B., 1663 to 1665, Judgments, and on pp. 153–154,

faith of Colonel William Evans,[1] the administrator upon his estate, and the guardian of his orphan son[2] (a point, upon which our ancestors betrayed the keenest sensibility),[3] as well as the god-father of his supposed daughter.[4] No fact, in his life,

there is a certificate of Doct. Thos. Gerrard's election, in 1652, to the House of Burgesses, over the signature of thirty-seven freemen, including Mr. Maunsell. Some of them had signed the Protestant Declaration. If Mr. Maunsell's neighbors could affix their names, why was not he, also, a signer?

[1] See Will of Col. Wm. Evans, the Roman Catholic, Lib. No. 1, 1635 to 1674, p. 331–332.

[2] Mr. Maunsell, it would seem, died about 1660, without a will. And his son John, then in his seventeenth year (in conformity, we may presume, with the faith of the family), "made choice of Capt." (subsequently Col.) "Wm. Evans, for his guardian;" who immediately afterwards received instructions from the Court, to "take out letters of administration." See Lib. S. 1658 to 1662, Judgments, p. 343.

[3] So great was the anxiety manifested by our ancestors upon this subject, that in some cases they provided, even in their wills, for a change of the guardian, upon his adoption of a different faith from that held by the testator.

[4] No freeman, or gentleman, who bore the name of Maunsell, had lived here, but the Assembly-man and his son; and from the relationship also of Col. Evans—the godfather of the one (see his will) and the guardian of the other child—we infer, that Mary was the sister of John, and the daughter of the emigrant of 1637. In an age of so much earnestness, we cannot believe that a Protestant would allow his child to be baptized by a Roman Catholic priest; or that a Roman Catholic would become the sponsor for an infant

weakens the inference; but everything, that is known of him, confirms and sustains it. Even if he were a Protestant; or we suppose, he was a delegate, either from St. Clement's, or from Newtown; he could still but represent the sentiments of the Roman Catholic party. Nearly all the inhabitants of the former hundred were the tenants of Doct. Gerrard; or the suitors before the court-leet and the court-baron held upon St. Clement's manor. For nothing was the latter more noted, than for the great number of its Roman Catholics.

receiving the sacramental rite from a Protestant. How natural, then, is the supposition, that Col. Evans, and the Assembly-man of 1649, were members of the same church!

CHAPTER XXXI.

Mr. Thomas Thornborough.

THERE is sufficient evidence to prove the identity of "Thomas" with "Mr. Thornborough," the Assembly-man of 1649[1]—to say nothing of the fact, that he was the only person of his surname, in the province, during that period. The first glimpse, we have of him, relates to the right, he held to "Mr. Neale's Plantation," the same, I presume, as "Wolleston"[2] (itself a corruption of "Woolstanton"[3]) Manor, surveyed in 1642, near the mouth of the Wicomico,[4] for Capt. James Neale, the privy councillor of Maryland, and the

[1] In some parts of the record, he is styled "Mr. Thornborough;" in others, relating to the same transactions, "Mr. Thomas Thornborough."

[2] Rent Roll for St. Mary's and Charles, vol. 2, fol. 283.

[3] The name of a town in Staffordshire.

[4] Lib. A. B. and H., p. 95.

ancestor of the second archbishop[1] of Baltimore. From some expressions in the deposition of Col. Jarboe, it would seem, he soon afterwards manifested a sympathy for Capt. Ingle, or the other enemies of the government.[2] But his offence is nowhere stated; we know but little, if anything, of its nature; although it is highly probable (looking at the subsequent Act of the Assembly) that the *original* ground of hostility had reference rather to the subject of a land-title than to the rightful authority of Governor Calvert.[3] It is certain that

[1] The most Rev. Leonard Neale, who died in 1817.

[2] The depositions of Col. Evans, and of Col. Jarboe, are of the same purport. "John Jarbo deposed, saith, that being at Kicetan, Mr. Calvert sent this deponent to Mr. Thornborough, to desire him to meet him at York, and speak with him; and bid this deponent tell y[e] said Mr. Thornborough, that he should not fear any thing, what had passed in former times, and that y[e] plantation (meaning Mr. Neale's plantation, as this deponent believeth), or any thing else that was formerly his (to wit Mr. Thornborough's) in Maryland, he would confirm it unto him. And, upon this, the said Mr. Thornborough came up with Mr. Calvert. And further, meeting him, the said Mr. Calvert, at York; he, the said Mr. Calvert, took him, the said Mr. Thornborough, by the hand, bidding him welcome; and, in this deponent's hearing, forgave him; and spake the former words of gift, or such like, to him." Lib. No. 2, p. 286.

[3] In case of Mr. Thornborough's attainder, or the forfeiture of a fee-simple title, the manor would have become, not Capt. Neale's,

a cordial understanding was re-established between the governor and himself, while they were both in Virginia; that they returned to Maryland; that the latter aided the former in the defence of Fort St. Inigo's, as well as the overthrow of the rebels;[1] and that he was the object of the most

but the proprietary's. Why should the legislature find it necessary "to stand betwixt" the grantor and the grantee, except upon the supposition of a controversy, which had involved, first, the captain and then the governor, before the meeting in Virginia? "Whereas it appeareth, that Nathanial Pope, attorney of Mr. James Neale, by virtue of his letter of attorney, gave unto Mr. Thos. Thornborough the plantation, which was formerly ye said Mr. Neale's, to enjoy for ever, upon condition y^t^ he would come into the country, and seat upon it. And whereas likewise there are divers depositions upon record, how that Mr. Calvert, late governor, did confirm what was formerly belonging to the said Mr. Thornborough, in Maryland, before his last coming into the province to reassume the government; and did give the said plantation unto the said Mr. Thornborough. We, the freemen assembled in this General Assembly, do generally and unanimously bind ourselves, to save ye said Mr. Thornborough harmless; and to stand betwixt the said Mr. Neale and him; whereby he, the said Mr. Thornborough, may go upon the said plantation, and enjoy the same." See Legislative Proceedings of 1648, Lib. No. 2, pp. 295, 296. The conveyance from Capt. Neale's attorney to Mr. Thornborough is not, indeed, upon the record; and it is impossible to say exactly what sort of title was transferred.

[1] For his services at St. Inigo's Fort, Governor Calvert gave him a "horse." Lib. No. 3, p. 43.

bitter hate on the part of the Protestant enemies of the proprietary.[1] He also sat in the Assemblies of 1648[2] and 1649.[3] Considering the period of our provincial history, when questions of a religious character formed the most important element in the composition of political parties; we do no violence to the evidence still accessible, in at least presuming,[4] he held the same faith as the governor and

[1] Col. Price, Mr. Thornborough, and Thos. Hebden, were specially "aimed at, and their deaths vowed," by the enemies of the government. Observe the hostility of Gray, as we find it, in the testimony of Edward Thompson, of Virginia, taken before the government of Maryland, the "18th January, 1646," O.S. "This examinant saith, that being at his house in Chickacoan, on Wednesday last, one Samuel Tailor, coming into the house, and being asked by this examinant, what was abroad, replied :—The speaker (meaning Francis Gray) had spoke once again; and that they, that were the chief cause of entertaining the present governor, were aimed at, and their death vowed (meaning Capt. Price, and Thornbury, and Hebden); but that there was a party, that would go over from this place (meaning Chickacoan), so soon as the governor is gone to Kent, or where else they can get an opportunity to go over; and would fire, and burn, and destroy; all, that they can." Lib. No. 1, p. 210.

[2] In the Assembly of 1648, he sat simply as an individual freeman. Lib. No. 2, pp. 293–294.

[3] Lib. No. 2, pp. 488–489.

[4] Nothing is more reasonable—a presumption not rebutted (as it is in the case of Col. Price), but greatly confirmed, with regard

the proprietary. Nothing is known of his family, or the time of his death; but it is not unlikely, he was a relative of Capt. Neale, the Roman Catholic gentleman, who "gave" him the plantation.

to Messrs. Thornborough and Hebden; for neither of them signed the Declaration, although the former, having business at St. Mary's (see Lib. No. 3, p. 43), probably went to the very spot, where that paper was drawn up. Of the latter's faith there is no doubt. See his deed to Messrs. Nicholas Causin, Barnaby Jackson, and Luke Gardiner, for the use of the Rev. Thos. Copley, and his "successors," Lib. No. 2, p. 533. I may also add, that the supposition of two Roman Catholics out of three colonists comes nearer to the ratio of the former to the whole population.

CHAPTER XXXII.

Mr. Walter Peake.[1]

It still remains for us, to notice the life of another Assembly-man of 1649; but one upon whose memory, is cast the shade of sin and shame; whose fate it was, under the stern laws of that period, to look forward, as the consequence of his own deed, to the forfeiture of all his lands,[2] and to the beggary of his children; and, about the sixtieth year of his age,[3] to suffer a felon's death.[4] The time of his arrival is not exactly known; but it is probable, he came in 1646;[5] and that, in 1648 and

[1] Spelt also Pake.

[2] "Considering the miserable condition of the orphan," "who no way shared in the guilt of the parent," the proprietary subsequently gave a new patent for St. Margaret's, to Margaret, the daughter of Mr. Peake, and the wife of John Noble. Lib. No. 17, p. 98.

[3] In January, 1664, he was fifty-five. See his deposition, Lib. B. B., 1663 to 1665, Judgments, p. 262.

[4] The patent to Mrs. Margaret Noble recites his execution.

[5] He brought his son, Peter, during that year. Lib. No. 2, p. 523.

1649 (when he sat in the Assembly,[1] apparently one of the most respectable members), he resided in Newtown hundred; as he certainly did soon afterwards,[2] and for a period of many years later. From his association with Governor Calvert,[3] we cannot doubt the sincerity of his attachment to the proprietary's government. There is also further evidence of his faith in the Roman church, derived from the fact, that he did not sign the Protestant Declaration; from the composition of the jury, which tried his painful case;[4] from his intimacy with many of the noted members of the Roman church,[5] from more than one of whom

[1] Lib. No. 2, p. 288, and p. 488.

[2] Lib. No. 3, p. 100; Lib. No. 4, p. 11; and Lib. F. F. 1665 to 1669, Judgments, pp. 651–656.

[3] Bozman, vol. 2, p. 640.

[4] If Mr. Peake were a Protestant; and the rule, in the cases of Robt. Holt and Parson Wilkinson, observed; the jury, in his case, would have been of the same faith. It seems, however, it was not a pure, but a mixed one. See, *e. g.*, the will of the juror, Raymond Staplefort, Lib. G. p. 265. "And so," says he, at the end of that paper, "I rest in God, and all his saints, and angels. Amen." Roman Catholics, it seems, never asked for a jury of their own faith.

[5] He was intimate with Philip Land, John Jarboe, Thos. Mathews, and James Langworth. See Lib. No. 2, p. 449, and p. 372; Lib. No. 1, p. 562; and Lib. No. 3. p. 201.

did his children, at different times, receive those gifts, which it was so much the practice of the early colonial god-fathers to present;[1] from the well-known Roman Catholic family of Peake, living in St. Mary's, as late as the American Revolution, whose ascent indeed cannot be clearly traced (such has been the destruction of our records), but who, we have but little ground to doubt, were either his lineal or his collateral descendants; from the names given to his children; and from the marks borne by the tracts, he had taken up. His eldest daughter was named after the Virgin Mother; his son, in remembrance of him who is regarded as the chief of the Apostles, and the founder of the universal primacy of the Roman see. The names[2] of his wife, of a

[1] See the gift from Col. Jarboe, Lib. No. 2, p. 372; and the one from Thos. Mathews, Lib. No. 1, p. 562. Doct. Mathews was probably the god-father of Mr. Peake's son.

[2] His wife was named Frances. Anne Peake was either his daughter, or his daughter-in-law. I am inclined to think, there were two persons of that name, besides his other children, Peter, Mary, and Margaret. Richard Lawrence gave a legacy to one of his children. See the will, Lib. No. 1, 1635 to 1674, p. 65. For the names of his wife and children, see Lib. No. 2, p. 372; Lib. No. 17, p. 98; Lib. No. 2, p. 523; Lib. B. B. 1663 to 1665, Judg-

second daughter, of a third member of his family, and of a friend, were, each of them, given to corresponding tracts, all of which had the prefix of *St.*[1] More estates were surveyed for him, with the Roman Catholic mark, than for Governor Calvert, for Capt. Cornwallis, for Mr. Lewger, for Doctor Gerrard, or for any other Roman Catholic colonist in the whole province of Maryland.[2] The evidence is conclusive.

ments, p. 226; Lib. No. 1, 1635 to 1674, p. 473; and Lib. No. 14, p. 82. Margaret was married to Henry Aspinall.

[1] St. Frances, St. Margaret, St. Lawrence, and St. Peter's Hill were, all of them, in Newtown hundred, St. Mary's County; St. Anne's was in Charles. See Rent-Rolls. He lived upon St. Lawrence, at the time of his trial.

[2] In counting the tracts taken up by Mr. Peake, I include St. Anne's, surveyed, not for him, but for Ann. Excluding that tract, his number equals Mr. Lewger's, or that of any other colonist. For Gov. Calvert were surveyed the manors of St. Michael and St. Gabriel; for Capt. Cornwallis, St. Elizabeth, and West-Saint-Mary's Manor; for Mr. John Lewger, St. John's Freehold, and St. Anne's, in St. Mary's, and St. Barbara's, and St. Thomas's in Charles; for Doct. Thos. Gerrard, St. Winfred, and St. Clement's Manor, in St. Mary's; for Thomas Simpson, three tracts, with the prefix, in Charles; for Thos. Mathews, two, in the same county; for Luke Gardiner, St. John's, and St. John's Landing, in St. Mary's; for Col. Jarboe, St. John's, in Charles; for Mr. Clarke, the privy-councillor, St. Lawrence, and St. Lawrence's Freehold, in St. Mary's; and for Mr. James Lindsey, St. James's, St. Thomas's,

At St. Mary's city, in the month of December, during the year 1668, sat the high Provincial Court of the Right Honorable Cecilius, the lord proprietary. Charles Calvert, the governor, subsequently the third baron of Baltimore, was the chief justice. Before the bar of this tribunal, appeared this Assembly-man, indicted for the murder of William Price,[1] by piercing him, with a "*sword,*" "on the left," "through, to his right side, under the shoulder;" and then cutting his "throat," to "the depth of three inches." His plea (the usual one in such cases) was *Not Guilty.* Thomas Sprigg[2] was the chief member of the grand jury; and Christopher Rowsby[3] (destined,

St. Philip's, and St. James', all of them in Charles—and two having the same name—four being the highest number, with the Roman Catholic index, taken up by any one, excepting Mr. Peake; for whom, I am inclined to think, St. Anne's also was originally surveyed (although the certificate cannot now be found), making a fifth.

[1] "By force and arms"—"feloniously, and of malice forethought"—"contrary to the peace of his said lordship, his rule, and dignity,"—are the words used in the indictment.

[2] A near relation of Gov. Stone, and the ancestor of the Spriggs of Calvert, now of Prince George's County.

[3] Stabbed in 1684, by Col. Talbot, the deputy governor. See Thomas's Lessee *v.* Hamilton, 1 Harris and McHenry, p. 192.

himself, many years afterwards, to die by the hand of violence), the foreman of the panel summoned to try the case. No technical objection is made to the indictment; no attorney appears on the prisoner's behalf; no testimony is offered in his defence; no witness for the proprietary, in any way, cross-examined.[1] The jury retire; but soon return with their verdict. Asking the court to say, whether the deed was manslaughter, or murder; they find he "is guilty of the death," but "was drunk" at the time, and knew[2] not "what he did." He addresses no appeal to the sympathy of the judges; he submits no objection to the form of

Respecting the governor's flight to Virginia, his conviction there, and subsequent retreat to a cave, in Cecil, near the Susquehannah, where he was fed for a long time by the falcons, a strange and somewhat interesting legend has also been preserved.

[1] I write from the record of the case. We have no knowledge whatever of any cross-examination.

[2] The verdict:—"We, the men of the jury, sworn upon the trial of the life and death of Walter Peake, do return our verdict specially in manner following: That Walter Peake is guilty of the death of Wm. Price, by wounding him, in several places of the body, whereof he died; that Walter Peake was drunk, and did not know what he did, at the time of committing the fact aforesaid. Therefore, if the court are of judgment, that it was murdor, then the jury do find it murder; but if not, then the jury do find it manslaughter." Lib. F. F. 1665 to 1669, Judgments, pp. 651–656.

the verdict; but still remains in silence. "The whole bench, then," decide, he is guilty of "murder." But neither against the decision of the court, nor the impending sentence of death, does he utter a word. Once, and once only, did he open his mouth. It was the moment after the sentence. Then, he "desired," as a favor (and the request was not denied), that "he" might "*suffer death before his own house, where he*" *had* "*committed the fact.*" Thus perished and passed away, upon the gallows, in the spirit of a Catholic penitent, after a life of toilsome, heroic sacrifice in the wilderness, one of the men so honorably connected with the most sublime and magnificent conception of the seventeenth century! *Pope Alney* was the name of his executioner[1]—the only fact, which gives him a claim to any place upon the page of our country's history.

[1] Convicted of cow-stealing—but the subject of a respite,—"several persons" having, "upon their knees," begged his "life" of the governor. See the last-named Liber.

CHAPTER XXXIII.

Conclusion.

THE result is before the reader. A word will be added, upon the general spirit, which distinguishes the era of Roman Catholic toleration.

For the purpose of depriving the Roman Catholics of the honor, to which they are so clearly entitled, skepticism has often united with bigotry, in the feeble and inglorious attempt to overthrow the facts of external history. It has not stopped there. Admitting, for the argument's sake, the accuracy of the preceding narrative; it has been busy in suggesting, with a cold-blooded malignity, a variety of imaginary reasons for the policy adopted by the proprietary. It goes upon the assumption, that man is mean; that he has no generous, or noble spring of action. Representing a philosophy, which ignores not only the charity of the Gospel, but the very life and soul of history;

it never records the performance of a good deed, without the assignment of a bad motive. And it has been sometimes asserted, but more frequently insinuated—insinuated, also, in the most crafty and sly manner—that the Calverts were actuated by considerations of a selfish sort—that the fear of offending the Anglo-Catholic king at one time, and the Puritans of England at another, was the real secret of the policy, for which they have been so much commended—and that, in giving the invitation to Christians of every name, less regard was felt for the *bona fide* principle of religious liberty, than for the purse of the proprietary, or for the success of an experiment conceived, and executed in the spirit of a mere money-making adventure!!

Policy, indeed, of an enlightened and honorable sort, has always been one of the elements of a good government. It is also admitted, that the province of Maryland grew, both in population and in resources, during the sway of the first, and of the second proprietary. A course of honor is not at all times attended with disaster; virtue is sometimes rewarded, even in this world; and a liberal principle of government is not necessarily unsuccessful, in its practical or commercial results. Is nothing due to the memory of Washington, for spurning the vain and visionary offer of a crown? Does a gentleman regard his honor, in a purely utilitarian light? Do the daughters of America, in protecting the purity of our hearth-stones, consider merely how impolitic is the sin, which leads them so swiftly to the chambers of death? Or was Mammonism, under its thousand forms, either of a gross, or of a refined sensualism, the all-pervading, universal genius of society, two hundred years ago?

The truth is, the ingenuous student is rather surprised at the small extent, to which the principle of a mere self-loving policy was carried. There is no doubt whatever, that the early Roman Catholics of Maryland were heartily opposed to the political party represented by the Puritans. Nor were they afraid to manifest their opposition. We have two memorable instances. They opposed them by a proclamation, in favor of Charles the Second, within twelve months after the passage of the Toleration Act. And they bravely, though unsuccessfully, fought them, at the battle near the

Severn in 1655. The governor, who issued the proclamation, had been a leading member of the Assembly in April, 1649. He was a Roman Catholic, it will be remembered; and a fair exponent of the views of the Roman Catholic party, on the question, which then divided the English nation at home. His councillors, also, had been in the same Assembly. And however impolitic may have been the course of Governor Green,[1] his very want of policy is the strongest evidence of the fact, that the administration of the proprietary's government was not shaped by any very great fear of the Puritans.

The most remarkable view of the whole era arises from the stability of the principle, the uniformity of the practice, and the unwillingness of the government to run to extremes in either direction. The case of Lieut. Lewis called for the prompt interposition of the governor; for the rule was plain. Equally plain do we find it, under the articles filed against Father Fitzherbert. Notwithstanding his indiscreet zeal, no respectable court

[1] Thomas Green was the acting governor, the latter part of 1649. See Bozman, Addison, and other authorities.

could have given judgment in favor of the prosecution. But how easy would it have been for a class of time-serving politicians to pass such a sentence, as might gratify the colonists, in the midst of their clamor. Considerations of policy, also, were then urged, but without avail, upon the proprietary.

Cases enough have been cited, upon the preceding pages, to show also (what is the most interesting fact in the whole of our provincial history), that freedom of conscience existed, not only in the legislation, but also in the very heart of the colony. It prevailed for a period of nearly sixty years; a real, active principle; and the life-guidance of many thousands. Cases of individual intolerance always produced a sensation[1]—the best proof, in the judgment of the historical critic, that they formed, not the rule itself, but (to borrow a popular expression) the very *exceptions* to it.

Let not the Protestant historian of America give grudgingly. Let him testify, with a warm heart; and pay, with gladness, the tribute so richly due

[1] See Depositions, in the case of Father Fitzherbert, and other cases already cited; also note upon the will of Mrs. Fenwick.

to the memory of our early forefathers. Let their deeds be enshrined in our hearts; and their names repeated in our households. Let them be canonized, in the grateful regards of the American; and handed down, through the lips of a living tradition, to his most remote posterity. In an age of cruelty, like true men, with heroic hearts, they fought the first great battle of religious liberty. And their fame, without reference to their faith, is now the inheritance, not only of Maryland, but also of America.

APPENDIX.—No. I.

EMIGRANTS FROM ENGLAND.

See Note 1, ante, p. 81.

The Hon. Wm. Burgess, the leading colonist upon South River (see ante, pp.72–73), probably from Marlborough, in Wilts, arrived in 1650; and, at various times, transported about one hundred and fifty persons, including the forefathers of several of the most distinguished families now living in this state. He was himself, through his son Charles, the ancestor of the Burgesses of Westphalia; through his daughter Susannah, of the Sewalls of Mattapany-Sewall, closely connected with the family of Lord Charles Baltimore; through his grand-daughter Ursula, of the Davises of Mount Hope, who did not arrive from the principality of Wales, before the year 1720; and, through a still later female line, of the Bowies of Prince George's, represented by Doct. Bowie, of Upper-Marlborough, in 1853.

Many, also, of the distinguished families of Kent came, about the year of Col. Burgess's arrival. The few only which can be named here, are the Ringgolds of Kent Island, now so honorably represented, as they have been for many generations (*see note 2, ante*, p. 194), by a large number of branches; the Hynsons, who also have many descendants, including two families quite remote from each other, at Chestertown, and in other parts of this state ; the Dunns, who are now extinct everywhere in America, so far as I can ascertain, in the male line, except the branch represented by James L. Dunn, Esq., of Reading, Pa. ; and the families of Wickes (see note to p. 79, also pp. 93–94), and of Leeds — the former having removed from Kent Island, at a very early period, to Eastern-Neck Island (where also is a descendant), and at present represented by Col. Jos. Wickes, of Chestertown, and by many other descendants—the latter also having left a large posterity in Talbot and elsewhere, related to several of the most prominent historical families of Maryland.

The Stones of Poynton Manor (see ante, p. 178), the ancestors of the signer of the Declaration of Independence, arrived in 1649 ; the forefathers of Charles Carroll, of Carrollton, another signer, about 1680 ; and the Pacas, and the Chases, a long time after the Protestant Revolution.

The ancestors of the Hon. Jas. Alfred Pearce were distinguished in the early judicial and parochial history of Cecil County. They came about 1670 ; and the Pratts (a family of planters, and the forefathers, I presume, of our other United States senator), about the year 1660. The latter first lived in Anne Arundel County ; and Thomas, the name of the senator, was borne by the emigrant, and by several of his immediate descendants.

A late senator, on the side of his father, General Benjamin Chambers, is a Pennsylvanian—the General, however, having before his marriage, become a resident of Chestertown, in Maryland. And the ex-senator, who resigned his seat in 1835, inherits, upon one side of his mother's ancestry, the blood of the Bohemian, who founded the colony in 1660 ; upon another, that of the Hawkinses, who arrived about 1655, and of the Marshes, who came as early as 1650. See p. 70, p. 81, p. 263, and p. 264.

The ancestors of the late Hon. Robert H. Goldsborough, descendants of a very distinguished family of England, arrived about 1670, at Kent Island. They are now represented by the Goldsboroughs of Myrtle-Grove, of Frederick, and of many other parts of the State. The very manners of this senator illustrated the gentleness of his blood.

The Tilghmans of The Hermitage, represented by so many honorable men, including the president of the constitutional convention of Maryland in 1774, and a chief-justice of Pennsylvania, arrived about 1655. They came from Snodland, in Kent; and their arms are: *Per fesse sa. and ar. a lion ramp. reguard; tail forked, counterchanged, crowned or.* The crest is *a demi-lion sejant sa. crowned or.* No family of Maryland has exhibited a higher proof of piety—of that piety which manifests itself, in the reverence and affection cherished for the memory of those, from whom we derive our earliest being and blood — a sentiment indeed, which forms the only foundation, either directly or through sympathy and association, of the true historical taste. They took up many tracts, including "Tilghman-and-Foxley-Grove," upon which Chestertown was subsequently founded, then held, if I mistake not, through an intermarriage, by the Wilmers of Kent. I regret, I have not, at this moment, my memoranda before me.

The family of Hawkins, first of Poplar Island, afterwards of Queenstown; one of them a judge of the Provincial Court, about 1700; another (Ernault), at a later period, the surveyor-general of the customs; arrived from Nominy Bay about 1655; but came from London, several years earlier. Through the Fosters and the

Lowes, they were connected with the family of Lord Charles Baltimore. They were also connected with the DeCourcys; and, through the Marshes, are the ancestors of the Formans of Clover-Fields; of the Tilghmans, of Hope; and of the Chamberses, and other families, at Chestertown. And they are connected with the Williamses, of Roxbury, through a resident of Baltimore—Elizabeth, the daughter of Matthew, having married the late George Williams; and left eight children, including George Hawkins Williams, of the latter city. Of John, the judge of the Provincial Court, the father of the surveyor-general, and the son of Thomas the emigrant, a very interesting memorial remains, in the possession of the vestry at Centreville—consisting of a large and massive piece of silver plate, in a noble state of preservation. A fragment of his son's tombstone may yet be seen, near Queen's-town; but the date of Ernault's death can be ascertained, only by a reference to the correspondence of Elizabeth, his widow, now in the keeping of the descendants of the Hon. Thomas Hands, at Chestertown.

The Thompsons, of Cecil, subsequently of Queen Anne's and of Kent, arrived about 1665. Col. John Thompson, the emigrant, is distinguished in the history of the early treaties with the Indians upon the Delaware; and held a great variety of offices, including that of a provincial judge at St. Mary's. He married a daughter of Augustine Herman; and left a son bearing the baptismal name of the Bohemian. *Augusta*, *Augusten*, and *Augustene*, the names of his descendants, are but abbreviations or corruptions of *Augustina* derived from *Augustine*. The Thompsons of Kent Island, including the clergyman, are some of the descendants of this emigrant. See also ante, p. 80. Col.

Thompson, it is not improbable, was related to the cousin of Col. Clayborne. See ante, p. 78.

The family now represented by Doct. Peregrine Wroth, of Chestertown, descendants (there is strong reason to believe) of the Wroths of Durance (a highly distinguished house), arrived about 1670. To this gentleman I have expressed my thanks, for the interest so generously manifested, in the success of all my researches.

The Sewalls, of Mattapany-Sewall, connected with the Hon. Wm. Burgess, and with the family of Lord Chas. Baltimore, came about 1660. Henry was the name of the emigrant. From the first, they were Roman Catholics. See also ante, p. 73, and p. 169.

The Spriggs, the ancestors of the late governor, came, it seems, from Northamptonshire, about 1655. Thomas was the name of the emigrant. One of the tracts taken up by him, was called Kettering, the name of a town in that county. Northampton was another tract held by him; and the family seat, if I am correctly informed, for many generations.

The Taneys (the ancestors of the present chief-justice of the United States), arrived about 1660, and lived in Calvert. Michael, which runs through so many generations, was the name of the emigrant. The noble part he played in 1689, has already been noticed. In the late "Lives of the Chief-Justices," and also in "The Southern Quarterly Review," it is erroneously said, that he held the faith of the Roman Catholic Church. See ante, p. 92.

The Tylers, of Prince George's County, came about 1660. Robert was the emigrant's name. They are now represented by the Tylers of that county, and of Frederick, including Saml. Tyler, of Frederick city, the author of several works, and one of the commissioners for the reform of the practice, in the courts of Maryland.

The Lowes of Talbot, and, it would seem, of St. Mary's also —the branch in the latter county being represented by ex-governor Lowe—arrived about the year 1675. They were closely connected with the family of Lord Charles Baltimore ; and came from Denby, in Derbyshire. Their arms are:—*Az. a hart trippant ar.* And the crest is *a wolf passant ar.* One of the wills at Annapolis points directly toward Denby. See also Burke. And I am inclined to think, Lady Jane Baltimore was a descendant of the family at that place. Lord Baltimore calls Vincent Lowe his "brother."

The Claggetts of St. Leonard's Creek, ancestors of the first Anglo-Catholic bishop of Maryland, came in 1671. Thomas, the emigrant, was the descendant, on his father's side, of a mayor of Canterbury ; on his mother's, of Sir Thomas Adams, a lord mayor of London, and a cavalier in the reign of Charles the First. Their arms, which were admitted and confirmed in the visitation of the heralds, are impaled upon the original seal of the bishopric of Maryland. And they have various descendants, in the male as well as female line, including Doct. Claggett, of Leesburg, Va.; Prof. Saml. Chew, and the Rev. John. H. Chew, of Maryland. Through a daughter of the third Thomas from Col. Claggett, of London, they are the ancestors also of the Davises, of Mount Hope. Their arms are:—*Erm. on a fesse sa. three pheons or.* For an impression from the seal of the bishopric, I beg to express my thanks to the Rt. Rev. Doct. Whittingham. See also ante, p. 99.

The Addisons of Oxon-Hill, the descendants of the family in

Cumberland County, and represented by Doct. Edmund B. Addison, by Wm. Meade Addison, Esq., and by many other living gentlemen, came about the year 1678. John, the emigrant, was a privy-councillor soon after the Protestant Revolution; but had opposed the revolutionary party. See also ante, p. 147.

I cannot give the year, the Dorseys arrived; but it was probably some time before the Protestant Revolution. Col. Ed. Dorsey, of Baltimore County (I presume, the emigrant), died about 1700, leaving a large number of children; and giving to his sons, Charles, Lacon, Francis, and Edward, all his lands on the north side of the Patapsco; to his son Samuel, a part of "Major's Choice," and his "silver-hilted sword;" to his sons Nicholas, and Benjamin, a part of "Long Reach," at "Elk Ridge;" and to his son Edward, his silver tankard, silver tobacco-box, and "seal gold ring." This is now one of the most extensive families of Maryland; and they are probably of an English original. Col. Dorsey, I presume, was the ancestor of the ex-chief-justice.

The Darnalls, of London, arrived about twenty years before the Protestant Revolution. Col. Henry Darnall, the emigrant, was the son of Philip Darnall, and a kinsman of Lord Baltimore. For the part he performed, in 1689, the reader is referred to the Narratives. See ante, pp. 87–100. He resided at The Wood-Yard, in Prince George's County; and, a later period, at Portland Manor, in Anne Arundel. He left many descendants; and his tombstone is at The Wood-Yard, now (as it has been, for several generations) in the possession of the Wests; and the most interesting family seat, I have yet seen, in Maryland. The vane upon the house-top, the wainscotted wall—the other relics, and memorials relating to the era of the Darnalls—are all preserved with the most studious care. I give this testimony, with a grateful heart. It is honorable, in the highest degree, to the taste and piety of the present proprietors. The Darnalls were Roman Catholics.

The Brents, the Neales, and other distinguished Roman Catholic families arrived before 1649 ; and are therefore not here noticed. In making selections subsequently to that year, I have confined myself chiefly to the Protestants ; for whose special benefit, the principle of religious liberty was extended, by the Act of the Assembly, to all believers in Christianity. Let the living sons of Maryland know something of the blessings enjoyed by their ancestors, under the beneficent government of the Roman Catholic proprietaries.

Most of the persons, whose arrival is sketched in this Appendix, held the right, I presume, to a coat of arms. But not knowing the fact, I have said nothing ; well assured, how many spurious escutcheons are now used in this country ; and fully aware of the danger of running into very gross mistakes.

APPENDIX.—No. II.

See ante, p. 80 and p. 107.

SETTLEMENT UPON THE BOHEMIA.—EXTRACT FROM HERMAN'S JOURNAL.

FROM the extract, it seems the colonists did not arrive till 1661. But there is evidence, *aliund*., that the foundation of the colony was laid in 1660.

"By letter, Sept. 18, his Lordship, in acceptance thereof, recommended the granting to the Honorable Philip Calvert, Esquire, then Governor—And was then supposed, the one tract to contain about 4,000 acres; the other 1,000 acres; good, plantable land—danger of *Indians* not then permitting a certain inspection, nor survey of that far-remote, then unknown wilderness.

"Whereupon, January 14, a Patent of free Denization issueth forth out of the office; and Augustine Herman bought all the land there (by permission of the Governor and Council) of the *Susquesahanoh* Indians, then met with the great men out of the Susquesahannoh Fort at *Spes-Uty* Isle, upon a treaty of *soldiers*,* as the old Record will testify, and thereupon took possession; and transported his people from *Manhattam*, now New York, 1661, (with great cost and charge) to inhabit."

* In the MS. copy, this word is very indistinctly written.

APPENDIX.—No. III.

See ante, p.152, note 1.

FAITH OF THE JURORS, IN THE CASE OF THE PISCATAWAY INDIANS.

I HAVE said, the first twelve, there is strong reason to believe, were Roman Catholics; but I arranged them, not in conformity with the record, but simply with a view to my own convenience. The following is the order observed upon the record:—

Cuthbert Fenwick, foreman; William Bretton; Nicholas Gwyther; John Steerman; Edward Packer; Richard Banks; Philip Land; Wm. Evans; John Lawson; Richard Hoskins; William Johnson; John Medley; Richard Willan; Henry Adams; Robert Cadger; John Nicholls; Daniel Clocker; James Langworth; John Thimbleby; William Edwine; John Taylor; John Harwood; Zachary Wade; and Thomas Sympson.

Three of the preceding jurors had been in the Assembly of 1649.

Most of the Roman Catholics are easily distinguished by a reference to their wills. See, *e. g.*, the wills of Philip Land, and William Evans. Richard Hoskins is the only one, of whom I entertain a doubt. But we have the best ground for the belief, that he was the same person as Richard Hotchkeys, of "The Cross," and whose name is written in a variety of ways—a very common thing, two hundred years ago. Edward Packer, for instance, was the same, it would seem, as Edward Parker, a kinsman of Mr. Bretton. See his will. In the index to the Land Warrants, on p. 17, for Lib. No. 1, Richard Hoskins, it appears, is spelt "Richard Hodg key;" on p. 622, for the same liber, "Richard Hodgkeys;" p. 136, for Lib. No. 3, "Richard Hodskeys;" in the oldest book of wills, "Richard Hotchkeys;" and, in the index to that book, "Richard Hotchkey." It is not improbable, that Nicholas Gwyther, a thirteenth, was also a Roman Catholic; although I have not included him.

Four of the Protestant jurors (Messrs. Steerman, Nichols, Clocker, and Edwin) had signed the Declaration. Capt. Banks, a fifth, had been in the Assembly of 1649; and it is quite evident, that Robt. Cadger was a sixth. See his will; and the one also of his son, Robert. John Lawson, in his will, desires to be buried "according to the canon of the Church of England;" and speaks of John Taylor, the *god-father* of his daughter, "Jean." It is highly probable, therefore, that Messrs. Lawson and Taylor, making a seventh and eighth, were both Protestants of the Anglo-Catholic type.

It would be unsafe to assert any thing positive, with regard to the faith of the remaining four, Messrs. Gwyther, Harwood, Wade, and Sympson; though it is quite probable, Mr. Harwood was a Protestant.

The result, then, so far as the investigation has been successful, presents twelve Roman Catholics against eight Protestants. Nor is it certain, that these eight (a point of the first importance) all lived, in St. Mary's, in 1653.

Excluding Messrs. Packer, and Hoskins, we have ten Roman Catholics against eight Protestants.

INDEX.

A.

A.

A.

B.

C.

C.

C.

H.

I.

I.

J.

K.

L.

M.

N.

O.

P.

P.

Q.

S.

S.

T.

U.

V.

THE END.

www.ingramcontent.com/pod-product-compliance
Lightning Source LLC
LaVergne TN
LVHW010221110826
845151LV00004B/1170

* 9 7 8 1 4 2 5 5 2 7 2 4 2 *